LAURENT MARIOTTE

ESSENTIALS OF FRENCH CUISINE

Translated from the French by Katherine Gregor

Hardie Grant

BOOKS

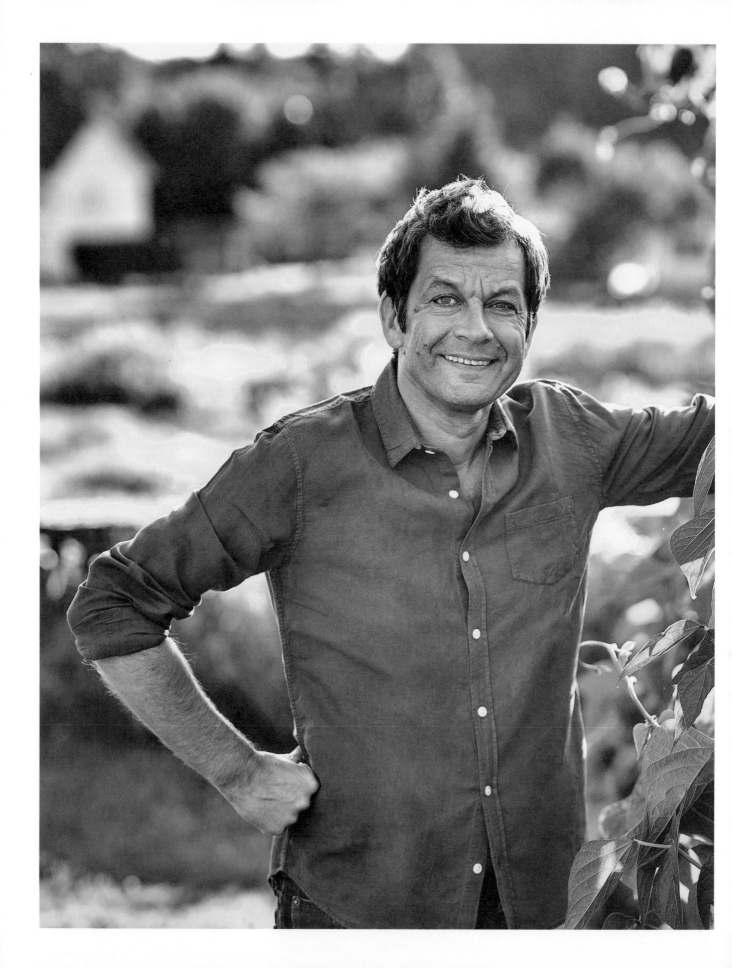

FOREWORD

—

Egg mayonnaise, veal stew, skate Grenobloise, chocolate mousse, tarte Tatin... Bursting with memories, these classics are essential to our enjoyment of meals. We've all come across them at one time or other at home, in a restaurant or at a friend's house. There's nothing like a dish to bring us together for a pleasant time. In this book, I have collected over 80 recipes from our French gastronomical heritage.

What I had in mind was a notebook of family recipes. These recipes are detailed enough to prevent mistakes and there are step-by-step instructions to help you with the ones you may find daunting. They are not over-simplified but specific enough so that you can make these classics your own. Chicory with ham, stuffed tomatoes, moules marinières... everyday cuisine is present and correct. Petit salé, boeuf bourguignon, sole meunière – classics sometimes forgotten await you. I have also included regional recipes like Toulouse cassoulet and salade Niçoise. To end on a sweet note, we have our pastry classics flirting with our grandmothers' desserts.

You have in your hands a concentrate of our culinary history. With anecdotes and memories, these recipes are much more than cooking – you'll see!

So let's get down to the classics, my friends – there's nothing more modern!

Laurent Mariotte

CONTENTS

STARTERS

ASPARAGUS WITH MOUSSELINE SAUCE

—

Derived from Hollandaise sauce, to which whipped cream is added, mousseline sauce transforms white asparagus into a treat.

—

INGREDIENTS:

16 white asparagus spears

few sprigs chervil to garnish

FOR QUICK MOUSSELINE SAUCE:

5 ml (1¾ fl oz/3½ tablespoons) single cream

150 g (5½ oz) butter

3 egg yolks

juice of ½ lemon

salt

1. Snap the asparagus spears 2–3 cm (¾–1¼ in) from the base. Peel with a potato peeler, tie in two bunches of eight with a string and plunge into a large amount of boiling salted water – standing up for 5 minutes, then lying down for 10 minutes. Drain then dab them with kitchen paper and arrange them in a dish. Keep warm to one side.

2. Prepare the mousseline sauce: whip the cream briskly and put it aside in the fridge. Melt the butter in a small saucepan on a very low heat, without stirring. Skim any foam off the surface of the butter with a spoon.

3. Put the egg yolks and 1 tablespoon of cold water into another saucepan. Whip while on a low heat until frothy. If it becomes too creamy, add a little cold water. Add lemon juice and salt.

4. Gradually incorporate the clarified butter with a small whisk. Fold in the whipped cream.

5. Serve the asparagus with warm mousseline sauce.

CELERIAC RÉMOULADE

—

Rémoulade, thickened with mustard and egg yolk, originally contains capers, lemon and shallots. These days, it looks more like mustard mayonnaise and is excellent with celeriac.

—

INGREDIENTS:

1 celeriac

juice of 1 lemon

2 eggs + 1 egg yolk

1 tablespoon mustard

250 ml (9 fl oz) sunflower oil

1 tablespoon white wine vinegar

salt and pepper

1. Peel the celeriac and grate it into fine slivers with the help of a mandoline. Sprinkle with 3 pinches of salt and the lemon juice, and allow to drain in a colander.

2. In a saucepan, boil the eggs for 9 minutes, then run them through cold water, shell and separate the whites from the yolks.

3. Mash the yolks in a bowl until smooth, then add the raw egg yolk. Stir in the mustard and oil to make a mayonnaise. Add vinegar and season.

4. Mix the celeriac with the sauce and chill in the fridge for at least 30 minutes before serving.

A WHIFF OF APPLE!

To lift this celeriac rémoulade, add some grated sharp apple (like a King of the Pippins) into the dish just before serving.

LEEKS WITH VINAIGRETTE

—

You can count the ingredients of this recipe on the fingers of one hand, though that takes nothing away from the enjoyment of it. Here's some bistro cuisine at home.

—

INGREDIENTS:

8 equal-sized leeks
1 tablespoon chives

FOR THE VINAIGRETTE:
1 tablespoon sherry vinegar
3 tablespoons sunflower oil
salt and pepper

1. Rinse the leeks and discard the tougher green leaves. Immerse in a large quantity of salted boiling water and cook for 25 minutes.

2. Drain and place in a serving dish.

3. Mix the vinaigrette ingredients in a bowl.

4. Pour the vinaigrette over the leeks. Chop the chives very finely and sprinkle over the dish. Serve the leeks and vinaigrette warm or cold.

ŒUFS MAYONNAISE

—

Are you familiar with ASOM (the association that protects œufs mayonnaise)? That's right: œufs mayonnaise is something worth defending, so I'm counting on you!

—

INGREDIENTS:

4 large fresh eggs

FOR THE MAYONNAISE:
1 egg yolk
1 teaspoon mustard
250 ml (8 fl oz) sunflower oil
1 tablespoon white wine vinegar (or lemon juice)
salt and pepper

1. Boil the eggs for 9 minutes, then run them through cold water before shelling.

2. Prepare the mayonnaise (all the ingredients must be at room temperature): mix the egg yolk with the mustard, salt and pepper. Add the oil in small trickles while whisking constantly.

3. Once the mayonnaise is firm, add the vinegar and whisk again.

4. Cut the hard-boiled eggs lengthwise and spoon the mayonnaise over them.

ŒUFS EN COCOTTE WITH HERBS

—

Eggs in pots are the ABC of cooking, and yet they are easily overlooked. My advice? Look the eyes in the eggs!

—

INGREDIENTS:

4 large tablespoons thick crème fraîche

2 tablespoons chopped herbs: chives, flat-leaf parsley, tarragon

4 extra-fresh hen's eggs at room temperature

butter

grated nutmeg

salt and pepper

1. Pre-heat the oven at 150°C (300°F).

2. Grease 4 ramekins with butter.

3. Season the crème fraîche with salt, pepper and nutmeg. Add the finely chopped herbs (keeping some aside) and distribute them equally among the ramekins. Break the eggs and put one in each ramekin without bursting the yolk.

4. Place the ramekins into an oven dish filled two-thirds with hot water, then bake for 8–10 minutes. Keep an eye on the oven: the egg white must be opaque and the yolk creamy.

5. Sprinkle the eggs with a little bit of herbs and serve immediately.

ŒUFS EN MEURETTE (EGGS IN RED WINE SAUCE)

—

Listed in our national heritage cuisine, eggs in red wine sauce are traditionally cooked in boeuf bourguignon leftovers so as not to waste the red wine and lardon sauce. Meurette comes from the old French word that means 'natural salted water', which is used for cooking our eggs.

—

INGREDIENTS:

2 shallots

2 garlic cloves

100 g (3½ oz) lardons

60 g (2 oz) butter

200 ml (7 fl oz) chicken stock

500 ml (17 fl oz) red Burgundy wine

50 ml (1¾ oz) white spirit vinegar

4 extra-fresh large eggs

flat-leaf parsley

4 slices French sourdough bread

salt and pepper

1. Peel and finely chop the shallots. Peel the cloves of garlic and chop one.

2. Sauté the lardons, chopped shallots and garlic in a large saucepan with 10 g (½ oz) of butter without browning. Add the stock and half the wine. Reduce the wine sauce to two-thirds over medium heat.

3. Prepare the eggs following the step-by-step instructions on the following pages.

4. Once the wine sauce has evaporated sufficiently, stir in the remaining butter, diced, and whisk to obtain a creamy texture. Add the stripped parsley leaves, salt and pepper.

5. Toast the slices of bread and rub with the remaining clove of garlic.

6. Place a poached egg on each slice, arrange on 4 bowls and spoon the red wine sauce over everything. Garnish with a sprig of parsley and serve immediately.

1

In a saucepan, start simmering
1 litre (34 fl oz) of water and the
remaining wine and vinegar.

2

Break an egg into a cup, pour it
carefully into the gently simmering
liquid and cook for 4 minutes,
turning it over with a wooden
spoon.

3

Remove it from the liquid with a slotted spoon and immerse in cold water to stop it from cooking further.

4

Drain it on some kitchen paper. Cut around the egg with scissors to give it a regular shape. Repeat this procedure with the other eggs.

ONION SOUP

—

Onion soup au gratin was originally served in the belly of Paris and Montmartre. Very popular among porters of Les Halles market and night owls after a sleepless night.
It is THE autumn–winter soup.

—

INGREDIENTS:

600 g (1 lb 5 oz) yellow onions
40 g (1½ oz) butter
1 teaspoon salt
½ teaspoon cracked
black pepper
8 slices of toasted baguette
160 g (5½ oz) grated Gruyère

1. Peel and chop the onions finely.

2. Melt the butter in a saucepan on a low heat. Add the onions, cover and cook for 10 minutes, stirring every now and then.

3. Remove the lid and cook for a further 15 minutes, stirring regularly.

4. Boil 1.3 litres (40 fl oz) of water. Pour 1 ladle of boiling water into the pan and stir briskly. Add the remaining water and simmer for 15-20 minutes, until a quarter of the soup has evaporated. Add salt and pepper.

5. Pour the soup into 4 heat-proof bowls. Add two slices of bread to every bowl, sprinkle with grated Gruyère and place under the oven grill until brown.

6. Enjoy this soup nice and hot.

POTAGE PARMENTIER (OR LEEK AND POTATO SOUP)

—

Like cottage pie, Parmentier soup contains… potatoes.
Thanks go to Antoine Parmentier, the pharmacist and agronomist
who popularised this nightshade in the 18th century.
This soup is a homage to him.

—

INGREDIENTS:

1 kg (2 lb 4 oz) potatoes

2 leeks (the white part)

1 onion

30 g (1 oz) butter

1.5 litres (51 fl oz) chicken stock

100 ml (3½ fl oz) pouring cream

walnut oil

croutons made with toasted sandwich bread

4 sprigs chervil

salt and pepper

1. Peel the potatoes and dice them. Clean the leeks, peel the onion and slice them all finely.

2. In a covered saucepan, melt the butter, leeks and onion for 5 minutes.

3. Add the potatoes, stir and pour in the chicken stock. Season with salt and pepper and cook over medium heat, half covered, for 25 minutes.

4. Blend the mix, then stir in the cream with a spoon.

5. Serve the soup in bowls, drizzle over a few drops of walnut oil, a few croutons, and some chervil and enjoy hot.

SERVES:
6-8

PREPARATION:
10 MINUTES

COOKING:
30 MINUTES

SOAKING:
1 HOUR

CHILLING:
48 HOURS

TERRINE OF DUCK FOIE GRAS

INGREDIENTS:

500 g (1 lb 2 oz) lobe of fresh, deveined, duck foie gras

200 ml (7 fl oz) milk

6 g (¾ oz) salt

3 g (½ teaspoon) ground white pepper

1 pinch of caster (superfine) sugar

40 ml (1¾ oz) cognac

1. Let the foie gras disgorge in the milk and 200 ml (7 fl oz) of water for 1 hour, to eliminate potential traces of blood.

2. Pre-heat the oven to 150°C (300°F).

3. Drain the foie gras on kitchen paper. Mix the salt, pepper and sugar. Spray the liver with cognac and season it with the salt, pepper and sugar.

4. Press the foie gras into a terrine of the same size and cook on a double boiler for about 30 minutes (the core temperature must be around 50°C/120°F). Gently pour the fat and cooking juice into another container. When the fat rises back to the surface, skim it and pour it back on the foie gras.

5. Allow to cool at room temperature, place a weight on the terrine so it looks smooth, then chill in the fridge for 48 hours minimum before serving.

6. This terrine will keep in the fridge for 3 weeks maximum.

CHEESE SOUFFLÉ

—

I promise you will master the art of the soufflé if you follow this recipe. Don't forget the golden rule: it's not the soufflé that waits but the guests!

—

INGREDIENTS:

3 eggs + 1 yolk

30 g (1 oz) butter + a little for greasing the baking tins

30 g (1 oz) flour + a little for the tins

200 ml (7 fl oz) milk

60 g (2 oz) grated Comté or Emmental cheese

1 pinch cayenne pepper

1 pinch grated nutmeg

salt and pepper

EQUIPMENT:

4 soufflé ramekins

THE PERFECT SOUFFLÉ

To ensure that your soufflé rises nice and tall and even, grease the ramekins without leaving finger marks, from the bottom upwards, preferably using a brush.

1. Pre-heat the oven to 180°C (350°F).

2. Separate the egg whites from the yolks. Put the 3 whites and the 4 yolks aside.

3. In a saucepan, melt the butter on a low heat, add the flour and whisk. Allow it to froth up but don't let it brown, then let it cool down.

4. In another saucepan, heat the milk with 200 ml (7 fl oz) of water. Pour into the flour–butter mixture (known as 'roux') and cook the béchamel sauce for 5–6 minutes, whisking constantly.

5. As soon as the mixture becomes creamy, remove the pan from the heat and add 1 pinch of salt. Let it cool, stir in the egg yolks, slightly beaten, then the grated cheese. Season with salt and pepper, then add the cayenne pepper and nutmeg.

6. Whip the egg whites until you have soft peaks and gradually fold them in with a spatula, lifting gently so they don't collapse.

7. Grease the four ramekins and dust them with flour (tap on the bottom to eliminate excess flour) and fill them up to three-quarters with the mixture.

8. Place at the bottom of the oven to stop the crust from forming too quickly. Bake for 25 minutes and serve immediately.

HERRING WITH POTATOES AND OIL

—

A bistro classic, herring with potatoes and oil is a staple on the northern coast of France. Prepared in advance, it deserves to be served with a side of warm potatoes.

—

INGREDIENTS:

1 carrot

1 red onion

4 fillets fresh herring

2 tablespoon black peppercorns

3 bay leaves

sunflower oil

wine vinegar

8 medium-size potatoes (Charlotte, for instance)

salt and pepper

1. The day before, peel the carrot and onion and slice finely.

2. Arrange the herring fillets in a deep dish, cover them with the chopped vegetables, peppercorns and bay leaves. Cover them in oil and a trickle of vinegar. Cover with cling film (plastic wrap) and marinate in the fridge for 12–24 hours.

3. On the day, peel and wash the potatoes. Immerse them in a pan of boiling water for 20 minutes, then drain and season with salt and pepper.

4. Cut the potatoes into rounds, distribute them on the plates, arrange the herring fillets on top and enjoy.

MACKERELS IN WHITE WINE

INGREDIENTS:

4 gutted mackerels with heads removed

2 carrots

1 onion

500 ml (17 fl oz) dry white wine

5 cloves

½ teaspoon crushed black peppercorns

3 sprigs fresh thyme

3 bay leaves

1 lemon

150 ml (5 fl oz) white spirit vinegar

salt

1. Salt the mackerels and put them in the fridge while preparing the marinade.

2. Peel the carrots and onion, then cut into thin rounds.

3. In a large saucepan, heat the white wine, carrots, onions, cloves, pepper, thyme and bay leaves for 10 minutes.

4. Wash the lemon and cut it into thin rounds. Immerse into the white wine, add the vinegar and cook for a further 5 minutes.

5. Wipe the mackerels, place them into the pan and simmer for 3 minutes covered, then turn off the heat.

6. Arrange the mackerels top to tail in a deep dish and cover them with the marinade. Allow to cool before putting the dish in the fridge for at least 8 hours.

QUICHE LORRAINE

—

*As a native of Lorraine, I give you here the authentic family recipe.
I can't repeat it often enough: no cheese!*

—

INGREDIENTS:

**1 homemade shortcrust
pastry (page 236) or
300 g (10 oz) pure butter
shortcrust pastry**

**250 g (9 oz) lean streaky
bacon**

10 g (½ oz) butter

6 eggs

**400 ml (14 fl oz) thick crème
fraîche**

salt and pepper

1. Make the shortcrust pastry following the recipe
   on page 236.

2. Pre-heat the oven to 200°C (400°F).

3. Immerse the bacon in a pan of cold water, bring to simmer,
   skim and cook for 2 minutes. Rinse the bacon in cold water
   to cool it, let it drain on some kitchen paper and cut into
   lardons.

4. In a frying pan, brown the lardons in butter until they turn
   slightly golden. Drain.

5. Roll out the shortcrust pastry into a circle of 26 cm
   (10¼ in) in diameter, about 3 mm (¼ in) thick. Grease
   a 22 cm (8¼ in) tin and line it with the pastry. Prick
   with a fork and distribute the lardons on it evenly.

6. Prepare the *migaine*: beat the eggs with the crème fraîche
   until everything has blended well. Season with salt and
   pepper and pour the mixture on the lardons. Bake for
   10 minutes then reduce the temperature to 180°C (350°F)
   and continue to bake for a further 20–25 minutes.

7. Allow to cool outside the oven for 5 minutes and serve
   the quiche with a crisp green salad.

WORD OF THE DISH

Migaine is what in Lorraine
you call the mixture of
eggs and crème fraîche.
Everywhere else in France,
this mix is called *appareil.*

PISSALADIÈRE

—

The pissaladière is named after the pissala, a paste made from very young fish macerated in salt and aromas for several months. This is hard to find these days, so I recommend you opt for good-quality salted anchovies instead.

—

INGREDIENTS:

1 homemade pizza dough
(page 236)

4 large onions

12 black Nice or Taggiasca
olives

4 fillets anchovies in oil

olive oil

1. Prepare the pizza dough following the recipe on page 236.

2. Pre-heat the oven to 220°C (425°F).

3. Peel the onions, cut them in half, then slice finely.

4. Drizzle a little olive oil into a non-stick frying pan and set over a medium heat. Add the onions and 2 tablespoons of water. Sauté for 10 minutes or so, stirring regularly until they start to brown and the water has evaporated completely.

5. Roll out the dough into a circle about 30 cm (12 in) in diameter and 0.5 cm (¼ in) thick on a baking tray covered with greaseproof paper. Spread the onions evenly, scatter with the drained olives and arrange the anchovies.

6. Bake for about 15 minutes.

7. Serve with seasonal crudités.

SERVES:
4 (30-50 GOUGÈRES)

PREPARATION:
15 MINUTES

COOKING:
20-25 MINUTES

GOUGÈRES

—

Ideal with an aperitif, these golden choux puffs are probably originally from Burgundy. The village of Flogny-la-Chapelle, in the Yonne, is the self-proclaimed 'world capital of gougères' as a homage to the baker Liénard, who allegedly invented them circa 1800.

—

INGREDIENTS:

250 ml (8 fl oz) milk

120 g (4½ oz) butter, cut into pieces

150 g (5½ oz) flour

5 eggs

grated nutmeg

150 g (5½ oz) grated Comté cheese

salt and pepper

1. Pre-heat the oven to 170°C (340°F).

2. Pour the milk into a saucepan and set over a low heat, and add the butter, salt and nutmeg.

3. Once the butter has melted, add all the flour at once, stirring constantly, with a wooden spoon, until it forms a smooth paste.

4. Let the dough cook out on the heat for 1 minute.

5. Take off the heat and immediately add 4 eggs, stirring. Add the pepper.

6. Pour the choux pastry into a piping bag or sausage filler. Squeeze the gougères onto a greased baking tray about 2 cm (¾ in) apart. Beat the remaining egg and brush over the gougères. Sprinkle with the grated cheese and bake for 15–20 minutes, making sure you do not open the door while they are baking. Serve immediately.

MAIN COURSES

SALMON IN BEURRE BLANC

—

Beurre blanc also known as beurre nantais leads you into the world of sauces. A staple in French cuisine.

—

INGREDIENTS:

4 leeks

30 g (1 oz) butter

2 tablespoons sunflower oil

4 skinless salmon fillets

salt and pepper

FOR THE BEURRE BLANC:

1 shallot

2 tablespoons white wine

100 g (3½ oz) butter, cut into pieces

salt

1. Cut the leeks into 1 cm (½ in) segments. Melt the butter in a saucepan over a medium heat, add the leeks and salt and pepper. Cook for 10–15 minutes until the leeks are soft.

2. Halfway through cooking the leeks, heat the oil in a large non-stick frying pan over a high heat. Put salt on both sides of the salmon fillets, place them into the frying pan and fry over high heat for 2 minutes, turn down the heat to medium and let them cook – without turning them over – until they are warm to the touch.

3. Prepare the *beurre blanc*: peel and chop the shallot very finely, put it into a saucepan. Add the white wine and let it boil down almost entirely. Gradually whisk in the butter pieces; the butter will become creamy. Add salt to taste.

4. Divide the leeks between 4 plates, place the salmon fillets on top and drizzle with *beurre blanc*.

GRAND AÏOLI

—

*They say that the Roman emperor Nero invented aïoli.
Whether or not it's originally imperial, aïoli is a very representative
sharing dish in southern French cuisine. So much so that it's even
served at Christmas.*

—

INGREDIENTS:

8 eggs

1 broccoli

1 cauliflower

2 fennel bulbs

8 carrots

8 medium-size potatoes (like
Belle de Fontenay)

1 litre (34 fl oz) stock

1.2 kg (2 lb 10 oz) desalted cod

slices of farmhouse bread
(as many as you like)

salt and pepper

FOR THE AÏOLI

4 garlic cloves

1 pinch of coarse grey salt

2 egg yolks

400 ml (14 fl oz) olive oil

juice of 1 lemon

1. Cook the eggs in a saucepan of boiling water for 10 minutes.
   Run them immediately in cold water and shell them.

2. Cut the broccoli, cauliflower and fennel into 2 or 4 parts,
   depending on their size. Cook all the vegetables separately
   in salted boiling water until al dente. The potatoes
   should be cooked in salted cold water and simmered
   for 25 minutes. Drain and keep all the vegetables aside
   in a warm oven (at 100°C/210°F).

3. Heat the stock. Cut the cod into 8 parts and simmer gently
   for 8 minutes. Drain and store with the vegetables, keeping
   the stock aside for the aïoli.

4. Prepare the aïoli following the step-by-step instructions
   on pages 50–51.

5. Place the vegetables, the eggs and the cod on a serving dish.
   Serve the aïoli on the side with lightly toasted slices of bread.

WORD OF THE DISH
Aïoli comes from the Provençal *ai* (garlic) and *oli* (oil).

1

Prepare the aïoli: after peeling the garlic cloves, put them into a mortar with the coarse salt and crush them to a paste with the pestle.

2

Add the egg yolks and mix with the pestle, adding 50 ml (1¾ fl oz) of olive oil.

3

Once the mixture is smooth, keep adding drops of oil. The mixture will gradually start to thicking and look like a mayonnaise.

4

Once the aïoli is thick and seasoned enough, dilute with 1 tablespoon of stock and the lemon juice.

MOULES MARINIÈRES

INGREDIENTS:

2 litres (68 fl oz) mussels (preferably from a mussel bed)

1 bunch flat-leaf parsley

4 shallots

60 g (2 oz) butter

10 ml (3½ fl oz) white wine

5 black peppercorns

1. Scrape the mussels in a basin of water and rinse them.

2. Cut the parsley coarsely. Peel and finely slice the shallots.

3. Melt 20 g (¾ oz) of butter in a large saucepan. Add the shallots and cook until softened.

4. Pour in the white wine and add the peppercorns. Simmer for 5 minutes, turn the heat up to high, add the mussels cook for 5–6 minutes until they open.

5. Use a slotted spoon to transfer the mussels into a pre-heated dish. Cover.

6. Away from the heat, add the remaining butter into the pan with the cooking liquid, stir and pour over the mussels. Sprinkle with the chopped parsley and serve immediately.

TROUT WITH ALMONDS

INGREDIENTS:

4 gutted and scaled trout

1 large egg

1 tablespoon milk

150 g (5½ oz) flour

20 g (¾ oz) butter

1 generous drizzle sunflower oil

125 g (4½ oz) almond flakes

juice of 1 lemon

salt and pepper

1. Rinse and dry the trout.

2. Beat the egg and milk in a deep dish and add a little salt and pepper. Pour the flour into a separate dish.

3. Heat half the butter in a frying pan with the oil. Coat the trout in the beaten egg. Flour them and tap on them to remove excess flour. Fry them on both sides until golden, then turn down the heat and cook for a further 10–12 minutes, turning them over once or twice.

4. Meanwhile, in another frying pan, sauté the almond flakes in the remaining butter for a few seconds.

5. Dab the trout with kitchen paper and arrange them on 4 plates. Sprinkle with the almonds and drizzle with the lemon juice before serving.

COLBERT-STYLE WHITING

—

When a cook decided to honour Louis XIV's powerful minister Jean Baptiste Colbert by linking his name to a breaded fish open like 'a wallet', this became known as 'Colbert-style whiting'. Moreover, this ensured posterity, since it was very flattering in those days to have your name associated with a dish.

—

INGREDIENTS:

4 whiting (300 g/10½ oz each)

100 g (3½ oz) flour

2 eggs

1 tablespoon sunflower oil

150 g (5½ oz) breadcrumbs

100 g (3½ oz) clarified butter (see instructions in mousseline sauce recipe on page 8)

1 bunch flat-leaf parsley

1 lemon

salt and pepper

1. Slit open the whiting through the backs down to the bellies without breaking them and remove the fishbone. Gut them, wash them and dab them. Add salt and pepper.

2. Pour the flour into a deep dish. In a separate dish, beat the eggs with a pinch of pepper and the oil. Put the breadcrumbs into a third dish.

3. Heat the clarified butter in a frying pan. Flour the whiting, avoiding the heads and tails. Coat them in the beaten egg, then the breadcrumbs, and fry in the clarified butter for 1–2 minutes on each side. Dab them with kitchen paper and arrange them in 4 warmed plates.

4. Fry the parsley leaves in the clarified butter and sprinkle them on every whiting. Serve immediately with a lemon cut in 4 quarters, with a side, for example, of steamed potatoes.

SKATE GRENOBLOISE

—

Before refrigerated haulage was invented, the fish that arrived in Grenoble was preserved fish, inexpensive and not particularly sought after. Grenobloise sauce helped jazz them up a little. And so it was adopted.

—

INGREDIENTS:

800 g (1 lb 12 oz) potatoes

1 unwaxed lemon

4 slices sandwich bread

flat-leaf parsley

80 g (2¾ oz) butter

4 skinless skate wings,
300 g (10½ oz) each

40 g (1½ oz) small capers

salt and pepper

1. Steam the potatoes in a steaming basket for 20 minutes, run under cold water and peel. Season and keep warm in the steaming basket.

2. Peel the lemon with a knife until the flesh is exposed: cut off the ends of the lemon and remove the skin. Hold the lemon in your hand and slide the knife on each side of the skin, separating the segments so you can remove the pulp. Dice the pulp.

3. Cut the bread slices into cubes to make croutons. Chop the parsley finely.

4. In two large frying pans, heat half the butter and sear the skate wings for 5 minutes on each side, then place on a dish, add salt and pepper, then cover.

5. Fry the croutons until golden in the other pan, then drain them on kitchen paper. Add the remaining butter and let it brown. Remove from the heat and add the diced lemon, capers and parsley. Mix.

6. Arrange the skate wings on four plates, sprinkle with croutons and drizzle with browned butter with lemon and capers. Serve immediately with the steamed potatoes.

SOLE MEUNIÈRE

—

In French, Meunière means that the soles are floured before being fried, basted with browned butter and brightened with lemon and parsley. I've watched chefs closely... The trick is in constantly basting the fish with melted butter.

—

INGREDIENTS:

8 sprigs flat-leaf parsley

4 soles (the black skins removed)

6 tablespoons superfine lump-free wheat flour

100 g (3½ oz) slightly salted butter

4 tablespoons sunflower oil

juice of 1 lemon

salt and pepper

1. Chop the parsley finely. Salt and pepper the soles inside and outside.

2. Quickly roll them in flour and tap to remove excess flour.

3. In 2 large frying pans, heat a third of the butter with the oil until the butter browns a little.

4. Fry 2 soles at the same time in two separate pans until golden, 5 minutes on each side, starting with the white skin side first. Keep basting with the butter.

5. Once the soles are cooked, place them in a serving dish, pour the lemon juice over them and sprinkle with parsley.

6. Melt the rest of the butter in a frying pan and, once it turns brown, pour it over the soles.

SCALLOPS AU GRATIN

INGREDIENTS:

8 scallops

3 leeks (the white part only)

1 shallot

30 g (1 oz) butter

140 g (5½ oz) coarse breadcrumbs

1 small bunch flat-leaf parsley

1 small clove of garlic

1 tablespoon olive oil

salt, *fleur de sel* and pepper

1. Shuck the scallops, remove the membranes (see pages 66–67) without tearing them off their shells, run them under a cold tap and dab them with kitchen paper. Arrange them on a baking tray.

2. Slice the leeks and the shallot finely and sauté them in a frying pan with butter for about 20 minutes, stirring, until meltingly soft. Add salt and pepper.

3. Put the breadcrumbs, parsley, peeled garlic, olive oil, a pinch of salt and pepper into a mixer and blend.

4. Pre-heat the oven to 200°C (400°F).

5. Put a few grains of *fleur de sel* and a twist of pepper on the scallops, arrange the leeks around them, cover with breadcrumbs and bake for 15 minutes, or until the breadcrumbs are golden. Serve immediately.

1

Hold the scallop in your hand, flat side up. Slide the knife into a small gap in the shell to prise it open slightly and keep the two halves of the shell apart with your thumb.

2

Scrape the top of the shell with the blade of your knife to cut the muscle and open it.

3

Pull on the membrane and stomach sac while holding the scallop and its coral down with your thumb.

4

Throw away the stomach sac membrane and keep the membrane cool to make a sauce later.

SALADE NIÇOISE

—

To respect salade niçoise, there are two golden rules: no cooked vegetables and no starch! The only ingredient that goes through a pan is the eggs.

—

INGREDIENTS:

2 eggs

6 tomatoes

1 cucumber

1 green pepper

4 spring onions (scallions)

1 garlic clove

150 g (5½ oz) tinned tuna

150 g (5½ oz) shelled broad beans

100 g (3½ oz) Nice-style black olives

200 g (7 oz) fresh anchovy fillets

1 tablespoon olive oil

4 basil leaves

salt and pepper

1. Boil the eggs in a large pan of salted water for 9 minutes. Drain and rinse through cold water and shell them.

2. Cut the tomatoes and eggs into 4. Sprinkle the tomatoes with salt. Cut the cucumber, pepper and spring onions into rings.

3. Rub the salad bowl with the clove of garlic, put in all the ingredients except the tomatoes, eggs and anchovies. Mix.

4. Arrange the three final ingredients on the salade niçoise, drizzle with olive oil, sprinkle with finely chopped basil and a few cracks of black pepper.

5. Serve at room temperature.

TOURNEDOS ROSSINI

—

At the beginning of the 19th century, in a Parisian restaurant, the famous Italian composer Gioacchino Rossini ordered a beef fillet with foie gras and truffles. Embarrassed by the richness of this request, the maître d'hôtel had this dish carried behind the other guests. And so the tournedos Rossini was born (in French, tournedos means 'turned back').

—

INGREDIENTS:

4 rounds of beef (150 g/5½ oz)

4 slices sandwich bread (brioche optional)

100 g (3½ oz) butter

200 ml (7 fl oz) madeira

4 slivers of truffle (about 20 g/¾ oz)

4 slices partially cooked duck foie gras (50 g/1¾ oz)

salt and pepper

1. Take the beef rounds out of the fridge 30 minutes before sitting down to eat.

2. Cut the bread slices into circles the same size as the beef rounds. Let them brown on both sides in a frying pan with 20 g (¾ oz) of butter, then put them aside on kitchen paper.

3. Add 30 g (1 oz) of butter into the pan and cook the beef rounds 2 minutes on each side so they are rare, constantly basting them with melted butter. Add salt, pepper and keep warm in a covered serving dish.

4. Deglaze the pan with the madeira, scraping the cooking juices with a wooden spoon. Allow to evaporate to two-thirds then blend in the remaining butter to thicken the sauce. Add the truffle slivers and coat them in the sauce.

5. Salt the slices of foie gras and brown them in a very hot frying pan 30 seconds on each side.

6. Put a slice of browned bread on each plate. Place the beef round on top, cover with a slice of foie gras and drizzle with the reduced sauce. Serve without delay.

KNIFE-CUT STEAK TARTARE

—

The word 'tartare' refers to the Tartars, a nomadic people who travelled across the steppes of Central Asia. They would chop the meat from their hunt and eat it raw. Even nowadays, real steak tartare is chopped with a knife, not minced.

—

INGREDIENTS

500–600 g (1 lb 2 oz–
1 lb 5 oz) beef (like rump steak
or tenderloin etc.)

1 tablespoon olive oil

4 egg yolks

1 tablespoon Dijon mustard

1 tablespoon ketchup

1 tablespoon Worcestershire
sauce

1 pinch cayenne pepper

tabasco sauce

salt and pepper

FOR THE GARNISH:

1 small shallot

¼ onion

2 tablespoons small capers in
vinegar

3 stems flat-leaf parsley

1. Prepare the garnish: peel the shallot and onion. Chop the capers, parsley, shallot and onion separately.

2. Dice the meat with a very sharp knife. Put it into a mixing bowl and stir in the olive oil and half the garnish. Salt and pepper lightly.

3. In a bowl, mix the egg yolks, mustard, ketchup and Worcestershire sauce, the cayenne pepper and the Tabasco. Salt and pepper lightly.

4. Stir the sauce into the chopped meat. Put a dollop of tartare on each plate.

5. Serve the tartare with the remaining garnish, homemade frites (page 164) and a crisp green salad.

SERVES:
4

PREPARATION:
15 MINUTES

RESTING:
1 HOUR

COOKING:
15 MINUTES

FLANK STEAK WITH ROQUEFORT SAUCE

—

A great bistro classic, the flank steak with Roquefort sauce is a charming dish, the way I like them. It has texture, a creamy sauce and people always have something to say about it.

—

INGREDIENTS:

2 thick flank steaks (200–300 g/7–10½ oz each)

120 g (4½ oz) Roquefort

200 ml (7 fl oz) pouring cream

sunflower oil

chives

salt and pepper

1. Take the steaks out of the fridge 1 hour before sitting down to eat.

2. In a very hot frying pan, fry them in a few drops of sunflower oil for 3–4 minutes on each side, depending how well done you want them. Cover and leave to let rest, adding salt. Immediately deglaze the pan with a few drops of water and leave over the heat so that all that's left is the cooking juices.

3. Prepare the sauce: dice the Roquefort. In a frying pan, let the cream and meat juices evaporate until the sauce coats the back of a wooden spoon. Add the Roquefort, whisk quickly and add pepper.

4. Pour the sauce at the bottom of a serving dish. Slice the steak and arrange on the sauce, then sprinkle with finely chopped chives.

5. Serve with homemade frites (page 164).

RIB STEAK WITH BÉARNAISE SAUCE

INGREDIENTS:

4 small rib steaks (2 cm/¾ in thick) or 2 large ones

1 tablespoon sunflower oil

1 knob of butter

salt and pepper

FOR THE BÉARNAISE SAUCE:

1 shallot

50 ml (1¾ fl oz) white vinegar

3 tablespoons chopped tarragon

½ teaspoon ground white pepper

3 egg yolks

125 g (4½ oz) melted butter at room temperature

salt

1. Take the rib steaks out of the fridge 30 minutes before sitting down to eat.

2. Prepare the béarnaise sauce: peel the shallot and chop it finely. Put it into a saucepan with the vinegar, 2 tablespoons tarragon and the pepper. Set over low until the vinegar evaporates, stirring regularly.

3. Away from the heat, add the beaten egg yolks and 1 teaspoon water. Whisk briskly, put the pan back on the stovetop on low heat and keep whisking until you obtain a creamy consistency.

4. Turn off the heat and gradually add the butter, constantly whisking. Pour the sauce through a fine strainer, add the remaining tarragon and salt. Let the sauce cool down until it thickens.

5. Cook the rib steaks for about 2 minutes on each side, so they are rare, in a very hot frying pan with the oil and butter. Salt, pepper and let them rest for as long as you've cooked them on a griddle or a plate turned upside down before serving with the béarnaise sauce.

BEEF STEW

INGREDIENTS:

400 g (14 oz) brisket

400 g (14 oz) shoulder

400 g (14 oz) chuck steak

1 onion

3 cloves

1 bulb garlic

1 bouquet garni

4 large carrots

3 small leeks

6 pieces of marrowbone

gherkins and mustard,
for serving

coarse salt and pepper

1. Cut the meat into large cubes. Peel the onion and stick the cloves into it.

2. Put the brisket into a large casserole. Cover with water and bring to the boil. Simmer gently for 30 minutes, skimming regularly if necessary.

3. Add the shoulder, chuck steak, onion, peeled garlic bulb and bouquet garni. Simmer for 2 hours 30 minutes, half covered.

4. Peel and wash all the vegetables. Add them to the casserole with the marrowbones after 2 hours 30 minutes of cooking. Cook for a further 25–30 minutes uncovered. Check how the vegetables are doing with the tip of a knife.

5. Serve the meat with the vegetables around it, the stock aside, and serve hot with coarse salt, gherkins and mustard. Add salt and pepper to taste.

SERVES:
4

PREPARATION:
25 MINUTES

CHILLING:
12 HOURS

COOKING:
3 HOURS

PROVENÇAL BEEF CHEEK DAUBE

—

The Provençal word daube allegedly comes from the Italian adobbo, which means marinade. This is why our beef is braised gently in its Provençal marinade.

—

INGREDIENTS:

800 g (1 lb 2 oz) beef cheek

100 g (3½ oz) smoked bacon

1 large onion

1 small unwaxed orange

4 carrots

4 garlic cloves

1 bouquet garni

2 cloves

1 bottle red wine (like Corbières)

1 tablespoon tomato purée

100 g (3½ oz) green Provence olives

olive oil

salt and pepper

1. Cut the cheek into large, 5-cm (2-in) cubes and the bacon into large lardons, and put them all into a deep dish.

2. Peel and slice the onion finely. Remove the orange zest with a peeler.

3. Peel the carrots and cut them into thick circles. Add them to the dish with the garlic cloves, crushed but still in their skins, the bouquet garni, cloves, orange zest and a drizzle of olive oil. Add the wine, cover with cling film (plastic wrap) and put in the fridge for 12 hours.

4. Pre-heat the oven to 170°C (340°F).

5. Drain and dab the pieces of meat (keep the marinade), then brown with a little oil in an oven-proof casserole.

6. Add salt, pepper, the marinade and the tomato purée. Bring to the boil, skim and put in the oven for 3 hours, covered.

7. Add the olives 10 minutes before finishing cooking. Let the cooking juices evaporate on the hob if necessary.

8. Serve hot with tagliatelle or steamed potatoes.

BŒUF BOURGUIGNON

—

How about a scoop? Despite its name, bœuf bourguignon was not born in Burgundy, but takes its name after the 'bourguignonne'-style wine sauce used in 19th-century middle-class cuisine.

—

INGREDIENTS

700 g (1 lb 9 oz) beef cheek

700 g (1 lb 9 oz) chuck steak

200 g (7 oz) bacon

3 large onions

30 g (1 oz) butter

1 garlic clove, peeled and left whole

sunflower oil

parsley

salt and pepper

FOR THE MARINADE:

1 bottle red Burgundy wine

50 ml (1¾ fl oz) de marc de Bourgogne (pomace spirit)

1 bouquet garni

5 black peppercorns

3 carrots

125 g (4½ oz) button mushrooms

sunflower oil

1. Cut the cheek and chuck steak into large, 5-cm (2-in) cubes. In a mixing bowl, mix the wine, marc, bouquet garni, peppercorns and 1 tablespoon sunflower oil. Peel the carrots and cut them into chunks. Wash the mushrooms and cut them in half. Add everything to the marinade then pour it all on the meat.

2. Cut the rind off the bacon and cut the latter into lardons. Peel the onions and chop them coarsely. In a casserole, fry the onions and lardons until golden in 20 g (1 oz) of butter and 1 tablespoon oil, then keep them aside on a plate.

3. In the same casserole, sauté the pieces of strained meat, browning all sides. Add the onions, lardons and marinade. Bring to the boil and add the whole, peeled garlic clove.

4. Cover and simmer for 3 hours on a low heat. Serve with steamed potatoes or fresh pasta.

DO NOT MARINATE ME!

After countless debates and essays on the importance of marinating the meat overnight, chefs and chemists have decided that the long rest added nothing and actually was likely to toughen the meat

BLANQUETTE DE VEAU (FRENCH VEAL STEW)

—

The first recipe for this traditional dish, with its white sauce, dates back to 1733. Back then it was used for leftover roast meats. We owe the current recipe to Jules Gouffé, who had the brilliant idea of poaching the veal before coating it in the white sauce, which inspired the French name blanquette.

—

INGREDIENTS:

200 g (7 oz) veal flank

600 g (1 lb 5 oz) veal shoulder

1 onion

3 cloves

1 carrot

1 small leek

1 small celery stalk

1 garlic clove

1 bouquet garni

salt and pepper

AS A SIDE:

15–20 small pearl onions

20 g (¾ oz) butter

1 pinch of salt

1 pinch caster sugar

FOR THE BUTTON MUSHROOMS:

150–200 g (5½–7 oz) button mushrooms

20 g (¾ oz) butter

juice of ½ lemon

1 pinch of salt

FOR THE SAUCE:

40 g (1½ oz) butter

40 g (1½ oz) flour

50 ml (1¾ oz) stock from the cooked meat

salt and pepper

1 egg yolk

100 g (3½ oz) thick crème fraîche

juice of 1 lemon

1. Cut the veal side into large cubes, place them and the shoulder into a casserole and cover with cold water. Bring to the boil and cook for 2 minutes then strain the meat, rinse it and put it into a stockpot.

2. Peel the onion and carrot. Stick the cloves into the onion, slice the carrots in rounds and the leek into segments. Put them into the stockpot with the meat and add the celery, peeled garlic and bouquet garni. Cover with 3–5 cm (1–2 in) water. Salt, pepper and simmer, covered, for 1 hours 30 minutes on low heat.

3. Prepare the side dish: peel the pearl onions, put them into a frying pan and half-cover them with water. Add the butter, salt and sugar. Cover with greaseproof paper and cook over low heat until the liquid evaporates.

4. Prepare the mushrooms: wipe them, cut them into four and put them into a saucepan with water. Add the butter, lemon juice and salt, simmer for 5 minutes and drain.

5. Prepare the sauce following the step-by-step instructions on the following pages.

6. Drain the meat, put it into a casserole, pour the sauce over it and add the onions and mushrooms. Heat for a few minutes on a low heat, stirring. Serve with rice.

1

When preparing the sauce, start by making a white roux: in a saucepan, cook the butter and flour on a low heat until it is white and frothy. Remove the pan from the heat to stop the roux from browning.

2

Make the velouté: pour the cooled stock from the cooked meat over the roux immediately, while whisking.

3

Put the pan back on the heat, bring to the boil and stir with a small whisk until the sauce thickens. It must be smooth and well blended. Add salt and pepper.

4

Just before serving, thicken the sauce: mix the egg yolk and the cream in a bowl. Dilute with a small ladle of velouté then, away from the heat, pour the egg-cream mixture into the velouté. Put the pan back on the heat and bring to the boil while whisking constantly. Add the lemon juice and season as appropriate.

CÔTE DE VEAU WITH CREAM AND MUSHROOMS

INGREDIENTS:

1 onion

500 g (1 lb 2 oz) button mushrooms

50 g (1¾ oz) butter

250 ml (8 fl oz) whole crème fraîche

1 tablespoon sunflower oil

4 thick veal rib chops

100 ml (3½ fl oz) dry white wine

2 sprigs curly parsley

salt and pepper

1. Pre-heat the oven to 100°C (210°F).

2. Peel the onion and slice it finely. Clean the mushrooms and cut them into thin slices. Sauté them for 10 minutes in a frying pan with 20 g (¾ oz) of butter.

3. Add salt, pepper, followed by the cream and stir. Keep aside in a dish in the oven.

4. Melt the remaining butter in the frying pan with the oil and cook the veal rib chops for 5 minutes each side. Add salt and pepper and put in a dish in the oven.

5. In the same pan, sauté the onion for 1–2 minutes. Deglaze with the white wine and leave to evaporate for 2 minutes. Add the mushrooms to the cream and stir.

6. Arrange the veal rib chops coated in the mushroom sauce and sprinkled with the parsley leaves.

VEAL LIVER WITH GRAPES

INGREDIENTS:

200 g (7 oz) Chasselas grapes

50 (1¾ oz) muscat wine

10 g (½ oz) butter

1 tablespoon sunflower oil

4 slices veal liver,
180 g (6 oz) each

200 ml (7 fl oz) brown veal
stock (page 232)

salt and pepper

1. Pre-heat the oven to 100°C (210°F).

2. Wash and destalk the grapes. Cut each grape in half, put into a mixing bowl and drizzle with muscat wine.

3. In a frying pan, heat the butter and oil over a medium heat for 1 minute. Add the slices of liver, cook them for 3 minutes on each side until slightly browned and medium-rare. Add salt and pepper, then place on a grid over a dish, in the oven.

4. Wipe the grease from the frying pan, add the grapes and muscat wine, and sauté for 1 minute. Add the veal stock and cook for 3 minutes.

5. Arrange the liver, grapes and sauce on plates and serve with rice.

SWEETBREADS WITH MORELS

—

Sweetbreads are prime offal. Here is a sophisticated recipe with morels, for special occasions. Morels are a kind of spring mushrooms, which can also be found in dried form.

—

INGREDIENTS:

600 g (1 lb 5 oz) sweetbreads

30 g (1 oz) morels
(fresh or dried)

milk (optional)

1 shallot

1 tablespoon flour

30 g (1 oz) butter

1 drizzling of white wine
(or white port)

250 ml (8 fl oz) thick crème
fraîche

salt and pepper

1. The day before, disgorge the sweetbreads in icy water.

2. On the day, blanch them in water (start with cold) for 3 minutes from the time it boils. Peel them carefully. Dab and cut into large chunks.

3. Wash the morels carefully if they are fresh. If dried, let them reconstitute for a few minutes in warm water and milk, then drain.

4. Peel and finely slice the shallot.

5. Lightly flour the sweetbreads and fry until golden in a large frying pan with the butter for 6–8 minutes. Baste them regularly with the butter while cooking. Keep them warm in a covered dish.

6. Deglaze the frying pan with the wine, then add the morels. Once the cooking liquid has evaporated, add the shallot and crème fraîche, salt and pepper, and allow to reduce.

7. Serve the sweetbreads coated in morel sauce with seasonal vegetables.

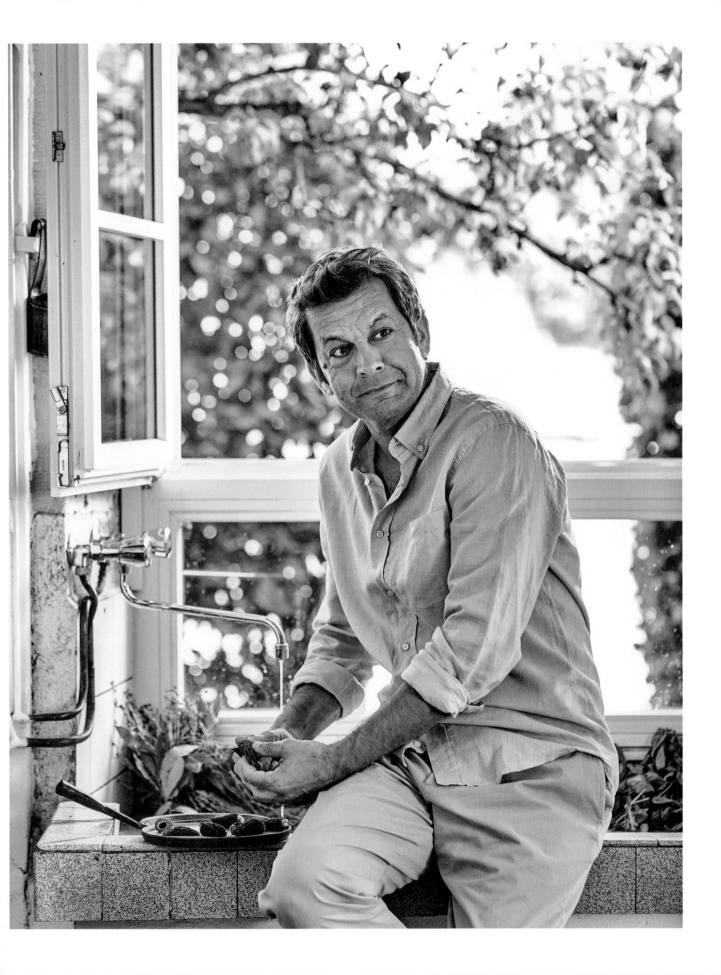

VEAL MARENGO

—

Chicken Marengo was created for Napoleon, who was then a general, after the victory of Marengo, a village in the Italian Piedmont, by his cook, using whatever he had available. The original chicken has been replaced with veal, considered more upmarket and tastier.

—

INGREDIENTS:

2 onions

700 g (1 lb 9 oz) sauté of veal (shoulder)

1 tablespoon tomato purée

2 garlic cloves

1 bouquet garni

50 ml (1¾ fl oz) white wine

750 ml (25 fl oz) thickened brown veal stock (page 233)

250 g (9 oz) button mushrooms

2 knobs of butter

4 slices of sandwich bread

1 tablespoons chopped parsley

sunflower oil

salt and pepper

1. Pre-heat the oven to 180°C (350°F).

2. Peel the onions and dice them.

3. Cut the meat into cubes and brown them in a casserole with a little oil. Add the onions and cook for 3 minutes. Add the tomato purée, stir and cook for a further 2 minutes.

4. Add the garlic cloves, peeled and with the germ removed, and the bouquet garni. Pour in the wine and let evaporate. Add the stock, salt and pepper, cover and put in the oven for 1¼ hours.

5. Meanwhile, rinse the button mushrooms and slice them. Sauté them for a few minutes in 1 knob of butter and add salt and pepper.

6. Cut large heart shapes in the bread slices and fry them until golden on each side in a frying pan with the remaining butter and a drizzle of oil. Dip the tips of the hearts into the sauce, then into the chopped parsley.

7. Arrange the meat in a serving dish with a slotted spoon, filter the sauce through a fine sieve over it, add the mushrooms, the bread hearts, tips up, and serve.

WORD OF THE DISH

'Escalope', in French, comes from escaloper:
to cut into more or or less thin slices,
on a slant.

TOULOUSE CASSOULET

—

Toulouse, Castelnaudary and Carcassonne all claim they invented cassoulet. Here is the Toulouse version, which contains several kinds of meat. All the recipes have in common the casserole or earthenware pot, after which this wonderful dish is called.

—

INGREDIENTS:

800 g (1 lb 12 oz) dried white beans

250 g (9 oz) fresh lean bacon

1 large carrot

2 onions

2 cloves

15 black peppercorns

250 g (9 oz) fresh pork rinds

6 garlic cloves

1 bouquet garni

500 g (1 lb 2 oz) deboned lamb shoulder

400 g (14 oz) lamb neck

400 g (14 oz) duck preserve in its fat

250 g (9 oz) Toulouse sausage

1 saucisson with raw garlic

120 g (4½ oz) breadcrumbs

salt and pepper

1. Soak the beans for 2 hours in a bowl filled with cold water.

2. In a saucepan of simmering water, blanch the lean bacon for 10 minutes. Cool it under a cold tap and dab it.

3. Peel the carrot and onions. Stick the cloves into one of the onions. Slice the carrots into rounds. Put the peppercorns into a muslin (cheesecloth) or a tea strainer.

4. Line a large saucepan with the pork rinds, the rinsed, drained beans, 3 peeled cloves of garlic, the onion with the cloves, the bouquet garni and the muslin with the peppercorns. Bring to the boil, skimming, cover and simmer for 1 hour.

5. Add the sausage and saucisson and cook for a further 30 minutes.

6. Chop the remaining onion and garlic.

7. Cut the lamb shoulder into large chunks and the neck into 8 pieces. Sauté in a frying pan in the fat of the duck preserve. Season with salt and pepper and put aside.

8. Sauté the onion and garlic and moisten with a ladle of cooking water from the beans. Simmer for 5 minutes.

9. In a second frying pan, fry the pieces of duck preserve until golden, without adding any oil.

10. Pre-heat the oven to 150°C (350°F). Grease a large earthenware oven dish or casserole (Dutch oven) with a little duck preserve fat. Arrange a layer of beans, then a layer of lamb and lean bacon, duck preserve, then sliced sausage and saucisson. Add the melted onion and its juice. Keep filling the casserole, alternating the beans and the meat. Sprinkle with breadcrumbs, add 2 ladles of bean cooking water and 3 tablespoons of warm duck fat.

11. Put in the oven and bake for 4 hours, adding a little bean cooking water halfway through cooking, if necessary. Use the back of a spoon to press the breadcrumb crust down several times during the final minutes of cooking.

12. Serve as soon as the crust is soaked in cooking juices and nicely golden.

PETIT SALÉ WITH LENTILS

SERVES
4

PREPARATION:
20 MINUTES

DESALINISATION:
2 HOURS

COOKING:
2 HOURS
30 MINUTES

Petit salé refers to this plentiful, popular dish from the Auvergne, in Puy-en-Velay, where green lentils originally come from, because of the salted pork it contains. Petit salé became well known thanks to Auvergne natives who moved to Paris at the end of the 19th century to open bistros.

INGREDIENTS:

1.2 kg (2 lb oz) *petit salé* (salted pork), cut into large chunks

1 garlic clove

1 onion

2 cloves

3 carrots

1 teaspoon black peppercorns

1 bouquet garni

1 bay leaf

1 Morteau sausage

400 g (14 oz) Puy lentils

1. Soak the pork in cold water to remove excess salt for 2 hours. Refresh the water twice. Drain.

2. Put the drained pieces of meat into a large casserole (Dutch oven), cover with cold water and cook over a low heat for 1 hour, skimming regularly.

3. Peel the onion and garlic. Stick the cloves into the onion. Peel the carrots and slice them into circles. Add the pepper, bouquet garni and bay leaf to the casserole with the *petit salé*. Simmer for 1 hour.

4. Add the Moreau sausage and cook for a further 30 minutes.

5. Rinse the lentils in cold water and put transfer to a large saucepan. Cover with water, bring to the boil, cover and simmer for 25 minutes.

6. Drain the lentils and the *petit salé*, remove the onion, the bouquet garni and the bay leaf, pour the lentils into a dish, and arrange the pork on top. Serve hot.

KIDNEYS IN MUSTARD SAUCE

—

Quick, affordable and easy to prepare, kidneys in mustard sauce are very representative of bistro cuisine. To enjoy fully, fry over a high heat.

—

INGREDIENTS:

2 shallots

500 g (1 lb 2 oz) veal kidneys

50 g (1¾ oz) butter

1½ tablespoons cognac

100 ml (3½ fl oz) brown
veal stock (page 233)

10 ml (3½ fl oz) pouring cream

2 tablespoons wholegrain
mustard

salt and pepper

1. Peel and finely chop the shallots. Prepare the kidneys: cut the white cores out, remove the nerves and cut the kidneys into 2-cm (¾-in) pieces.

2. In a frying pan, melt 30 g (1 oz) butter and fry the kidneys for 3–4 minutes on each side, so they are medium-rare. Season and put them aside on a plate.

3. In the same frying pan, melt the remaining butter and fry the shallots until golden. Deglaze with the cognac and set alight. Add the veal stock, cream and mustard, and simmer until the sauce has thickened a little. Put the kidneys back into the sauce and serve with gnocchi or potato purée.

SAUERKRAUT

—

The word sauerkraut *comes from the old Alsatian sürkrüt, from sür (sour) and krüt (cabbage). Why is it traditional to eat sauerkraut in Alsace? Because cabbages there are preserved in brine all winter, after being harvested in the autumn. Cabbages have been grown in that region since the early 16th century.*

—

INGREDIENTS:

350 g (12 oz) salted pork loin

300 g (10½ oz) salted bacon

1 salted pork knuckle

1.6 kg (3 lb 5 oz) good sauerkraut in brine (or homemade, page 112)

500 g (1 lb 2 oz) smoked pork shoulder

1 large onion

2 garlic cloves

50 g (1¾ oz) goose, duck fat or lard

1 bay leaf

8 juniper berries

2 cloves

½ teaspoon cumin seeds

1 teaspoon white pepper grains

2 rinds of bacon

750 ml (25 fl oz) dry white Alsace wine

4 medium-size potatoes

300 g (10½ oz) cooked, smoked bacon

1 Morteau sausage

3 Montbéliard smoked sausages

1 cervelas

3 Strasbourg sausages (knacks)

1 tablespoon gin

coarse salt

mustard (optional, when serving)

1. The day before, soak the pork loin, bacon and knuckle in cold water to remove excess salt.

2. On the day, rinse the sauerkraut in cold water in a sieve standing in water. Drain, pressing it. Rinse the desalted meats and wipe them with a clean cloth.

3. In a saucepan, blanch the piece of smoked shoulder for 5 minutes in simmering water.

4. Prepare the aromatic garnish: peel and slice the onion and garlic finely. In a large oven-proof casserole, heat the fat. Add the onion and garlic and sauté for 2 minutes. Transfer into a muslin bag (cheesecloth) with the bay leaf, juniper berries, cloves, cumin and white pepper.

5. Pre-heat the oven to 180°C (350°F).

6. Line the casserole with the rinds, with the fat side against the pan. Spread half the sauerkraut over it, adding two pinches of coarse salt. Place the muslin bag with the aromas on top. Add the raw meats (smoked shoulder, loin and bacon). Cover all with the remaining sauerkraut and one final pinch of coarse salt. Press slightly and moisten to the brim with the white wine (top up with water if necessary). Cover and put in the oven for 1 hours 15 minutes.

7. In a saucepan filled with cold, salted water, and add the potatoes: set a timer for 20 minutes from the time the water comes to the boil, then drain and peel the potatoes.

8. After 1¼ hours cooking, bury the smoked bacon and Morteau sausage under the top layer of sauerkraut. Bake for a further 30 minutes. Add, under the top layer of sauerkraut, the Montbéliard sausages and cervelas. Cover with sauerkraut again, pour in the gin and put back into the oven for 15 more minutes. Add the potatoes and Strasbourg sausages. Cover and allow the aromas to develop for 10 minutes.

9. Form a large dome of strained sauerkraut in the centre of a large serving dish. Cut the bacon into 1-cm (½-in) slices and the meats into chunks.

10. Arrange the cured meats elegantly on top of the sauerkraut and the sausages and potatoes in a circle at the foot of the dome. Serve nice and hot, possibly with mustard.

PREPARATION:
10 MINUTES

MARINATING:
30 MINUTES

LACTO-FERMENTATION:
1 MONTH

SAUERKRAUT IN BRINE

INGREDIENTS:

2 kg (4 lb 8 oz) white or green
cabbage

40 g (1½ oz) salt (20 g (¾ oz)
per net kg of cabbage)

1 tablespoon juniper berries

½ tablespoon black
peppercorns

1 tablespoon cumin seeds

1. Remove and throw away the top leaves of the cabbage. Do not rinse the rest of the cabbage (its natural bacteria will enable its lacto-fermentation), but wash your hands thoroughly.

2. Cut the cabbages into 8 parts and remove the core and the thick central ribs. Slice the cabbages finely into strips, possibly with the help of a mandoline.

3. In a mixing bowl, mix the sliced cabbage with the salt, juniper berries, pepper and cumin. Disgorge for 30 minutes.

4. Transfer everything into glass jars, compacting the cabbage, 2 cm (¾ in) from the top. Secure with the lid so they are airtight and leave at room temperature for 2–3 days, away from the light.

5. After 2–3 days, check that the slivers of cabbage are fully bathed in their brine. If they are not, add a mixture of boiled water and salt (10 g/½ oz) salt per 1 litre (34 fl oz) of water.

6. Keep the sauerkraut at room temperature for 1 month, always away from the light, before eating.

SERVES:
4

PREPARATION:
30 MINUTES

COOKING:
1 HOUR–1 HOUR
30 MINUTES

STUFFED TOMATOES

—

Let's not forget that there is a season for stuffed tomatoes.
It's the same as that of ripe, fleshy tomatoes: from June to October.
With leftover stewed or barbecued meat, stuffed tomatoes are inviting.

—

INGREDIENTS

4 large, ripe and firm
tomatoes (leave the stems for
presentation)

2 garlic cloves

2 shallots

1 small bunch flat-leaf parsley

60 g (2 oz) smoked ham

100 g (3½ oz) soft part
of the bread

500 g (1 lb 2 oz) sausage meat

salt and pepper

butter for the dish

1. Slice off the tops of the tomatoes 2 cm (¾ in) from the stem. Scoop out the insides, leaving a little flesh and keep aside the 'hats', the pulp and the juice.

2. Salt the insides of the tomatoes and place them upside down on a grid so they shed as much liquid as possible.

3. Peel the garlic and shallots. Chop them, along with the parsley, ham and bread. Mix it all with the tomato juice and sausage meat. Add pepper and mix until you have the texture of a smooth stuffing.

4. Pre-heat the oven to 180°C (350°F).

5. Fill the tomatoes so the stuffing overflows by 1 cm (½ in) and cover with the 'hats'. Arrange on a buttered dish and bake for 1 hour–1 hour 30 minutes. Keep an eye on the tomatoes; they should release juices, which you can use for basting the tops of the tomatoes.

6. Allow to cool before serving with rice.

SERVES:
6

PREPARATION:
30 MINUTES

COOKING:
30 MINUTES

RESTING:
10 MINUTES

ROAST LEG OF LAMB

INGREDIENTS:

1 leg of lamb

3 garlic cloves

3 sprigs of thyme

sunflower oil

coarse sea salt and pepper

1. Pre-heat the oven to 210°C (410°F).

2. Rub the leg of lamb with the coarse sea salt, put it into a roaster, add pepper, a little oil, the garlic, crushed, and the thyme. Roast for 20 minutes.

3. Turn down the oven temperature to 170°C (340°F) and turn the leg of lamb over, pour a small glass of water into the roasting tin and roast for a further 15 minutes.

4. Take the leg of lamb out of the oven, cover with aluminium foil and leave to rest for 10 minutes before carving.

5. Serve with Boulangère potatoes (see recipe page 160).

NAVARIN OF LAMB WITH SPRING VEGETABLES

—

Navarin takes its name from the turnip served with the lamb.
Traditionally, this dish does not come with green vegetables,
but I've decided to offer you a spring version.

—

INGREDIENTS:

300 g (10½ oz) deboned
shoulder of lamb

300 g (10½ oz) breast of lamb

300 g (10½ oz) neck of lamb

1 tablespoon flour

3 tinned tomatoes

100 ml (3½ fl oz) dry white
wine

1 bouquet garni

6 spring onions (scallions)

6 carrot tops

6 small turnip tops

3 garlic cloves

300 g (10½ oz) shelled petits
pois (700 g (1 lb 9 oz)
with the pods)

300 g (10½ oz) mangetout

olive oil

salt and pepper

1. Cut the shoulder and breast into 4-cm (1½-in) cubes and the neck into 6 pieces. Heat a large casserole with a drizzle of oil and brown the pieces of meat in small quantities at a time. Add salt and pepper.

2. Deglaze the casserole, return the meat to the casserole, dust with flour and cook for 1 minute, stirring.

3. Add the tomatoes and white wine and let evaporate for 1 minute. Cover with boiling water, add the bouquet garni and simmer over gentle heat for 30 minutes.

4. Meanwhile, prepare the vegetables, leaving 3 cm (1½ in) of the tops and the stems of the spring onions. Brush the carrots and turnips under a cold tap. Add them to the casserole, with the spring onions, then slip the garlic, in its skin, between the pieces of meat. Cook for a further 30 minutes.

5. Add the peas and mangetout and cook for 4–5 more minutes. Remove the bouquet garni and serve the navarin in the casserole.

SERVES:
4

PREPARATION:
5 MINUTES

COOKING:
23-28 MINUTES

RESTING:
5 MINUTES

FILLET OF DUCK

INGREDIENTS:

2 fillets of duck breast

salt

1. Pre-heat the oven to 180°C (350°F).

2. Score the fatty part of the fillets and salt them.
   Place them – on the side of the fat – into an oven dish.
   Cook on medium heat for 8–10 minutes. Deglaze the dish
   and cook on the flesh side for 3 minutes.

3. Put into the oven and roast for 12–15 minutes if you wish
   for the duck to be medium-rare.

4. Put the fillets on a chopping board and allow to rest
   for 5 minutes before slicing.

5. Serve with Sarlat potatoes (see recipe page 156).

VALLÉE D'AUGE CHICKEN

—

All the good produce from Normandy has come together in this convivial recipe. Apples, cream, calvados, cider – and hey presto!

—

INGREDIENTS:

500 g (1 lb 2 oz) button mushrooms

1 shallot

1 sprig thyme

60 g (2 oz) butter

1 about 1.7-kg (3 lb 12 oz) free-range chicken, cut into 8 pieces

¼ bay leaf

5 tablespoons calvados

200 ml (7 fl oz) brut cider

100 g (3½ oz) thick crème fraîche

4 apples (like King of the Pippins)

salt and pepper

1. Cut off the muddy ends of the mushrooms. Wash and cut into 4. Peel and finely chop the shallot. Pluck the leaves from the thyme. Salt and pepper the pieces of chicken.

2. Heat 30 g (1 oz) of butter in a casserole. Sauté the chicken over low heat, without browning, with the thyme and bay leaf for about 10 minutes.

3. Turn up the heat, pour in the calvados and set alight, lifting the pieces of chicken so they absorb it.

4. Add the mushrooms and shallot and sauté for 5 minutes. Pour in the cider, cover and cook for a further 30 minutes. Add the crème fraîche and stir. Season to taste and let the sauce reduce uncovered for 10 minutes.

5. Wash and deseed the apples and quarter them. Melt the remaining 30 g (1 oz) of butter in a frying pan and fry the apple quarters 10 minutes on each side.

6. Serve in the casserole, with the fried apple.

ROAST CHICKEN

—

It's the official Sunday family lunch.
To ensure your guests ask for second helpings,
you need to follow a few rules. Here they are!

—

INGREDIENTS:

1.8 kg (4 lb) ready-to-roast
free-range chicken

3 garlic cloves

1 sprig rosemary

2 sprigs thyme

2 tablespoons sunflower or
grapeseed oil

30 g (1 oz) butter

coarse grey salt

black peppercorns

salt and pepper

1. Take the chicken out of the fridge 1 hour before you want to cook it.

2. Pre-heat the oven to 180°C (350°F).

3. Crush the garlic cloves in their skins and slide them into the chicken, along with the rosemary and thyme. Add 1 teaspoon coarse grey salt and ½ teaspoon peppercorns.

4. Salt and pepper the entire surface of the chicken. Drizzle it with oil and put a few pieces of butter on it.

5. Put the chicken, breast-side down, into a roasting dish and roast on the top shelf of the oven initially for 45 minutes, basting it every 15 minutes.

6. Turn the chicken on its back, baste and put it back in the oven for 45 minutes, basting it every 15 minutes.

7. Take the chicken out of the oven. Deglaze the dish slightly and let the chicken rest 'head down' for 15 minutes, covered in greaseproof paper lined with aluminium foil, so that the juice spreads nicely through all the flesh.

8. Carve the chicken following the instructions on pages 134–135. Remove the herbs and garlic and serve immediately in a baking dish with its juice. Serve with boiled new potatoes.

1

Start by taking off the thigh by cutting the skin between the side and the thigh. Turn the bone that secures the thigh to the carcass around to separate them. Do the same with the other thigh.

2

Start from the keel and follow the breastbone to detach the supremes from the carcass, one by one. Separate the wings from the breast.

3

You can cut the tip of the wing off and serve only the cuff (but keep the tip to make stock, for instance). You now have a chicken cut into 6 pieces.

4

To arve it into 8, cut the thigh between the actual thigh and the drumstick. Don't forget the oysters on the carcass!

SERVES:
4

PREPARATION:
15 MINUTES

COOKING:
25 MINUTES

RESTING:
10 MINUTES

FILET MIGNON WITH SMALL SPRING VEGETABLES

INGREDIENTS:

8 green asparagus spears

8–12 pink radishes

4 spring onions (scallions)

100 g (3½ oz) mangetout

700 g (1 lb 9 oz) veal filet mignon

olive oil

1 sprig fresh thyme

6 small garlic cloves

salt and pepper

1. Pre-heat the oven to 180°C (350°F).

2. Wash the vegetables. Peel the asparagus. Cut the tops from the radishes, then cut the latter in half lengthwise. Cut the asparagus and spring onions into segments.

3. Brown the filet mignon all over in a sauté pan with a few drops of oil, the thyme and the garlic cloves in their skins.

4. Arrange all the vegetables around the meat, add salt and pepper and move them in the cooking fat. Put in the oven for 15 minutes.

5. Remove the filet mignon and set aside on a dish for 8–10 minutes. Leave the vegetables in the oven during this time.

6. Once again, coat the vegetables in the cooking juices and share them among 4 plates. Add the slices of filet mignon, drizzle with the cooking juice and serve immediately.

STUFFED CABBAGE

—

The ultimate people's dish, stuffed cabbage comes in a thousand and one versions. Here is my take on it, in its simplest cabbage leaf outfit, inexpensive and easy to make.

—

INGREDIENTS:

1 Savoy cabbage

2 slices sandwich bread

100 ml (3½ fl oz) milk

2 garlic cloves

2 shallots

10 sprigs flat-leaf parsley

1 egg

300 g (10½ oz) sausage meat

200 g (7 oz) slightly salted pork belly

1 litre (34 fl oz) chicken stock

salt and pepper

1. Throw away the outer leaves of the cabbage if they are hard. Remove 8 large leaves, blanch them, two at a time, in a large saucepan of salted boiling water for 4 minutes. Cool them under a cold tap to stop them from overcooking. Thin down the thick central stalks.

2. Thinly slice the heart of the cabbage and let it wilt in a casserole over a medium heat for 5 minutes.

3. Pre-heat the oven to 200°C (400°F).

4. Prepare the stuffing: soak the bread in the milk. Peel and chop the shallots and put them into a mixing bowl. Finely chop the parsley and add it, with the egg, to the garlic-shallot mix. Drain the bread and add it along with the sausage meat, the cooked heart of the cabbage and 50 g (1¾ oz) diced pork belly. Add salt and pepper.

5. Arrange the cabbage leaves on a worktop. Divide the stuffing into 8 equal-size balls, fill the cabbage leaves and tie them with string into parcels.

6. Put the stuffed cabbage leaves into a casserole, add the remaining diced pork belly all around and pour in the stock. Cover and bake for 25–30 minutes. Serve the stuffed cabbage with cooked rice.

CROQUE-MONSIEUR

—

This sandwich was created in the Opéra district in Paris, in 1910, for hungry audiences and workers when there were no baguette sandwiches. This recipe is over a century old and is still a treat.

—

INGREDIENTS:

8 large slices of bread from a baker's loaf

50 g (1¾ oz) butter at room temperature

2 large slices cooked ham

100 g (3½ oz) grated Gruyère

FOR THE BÉCHAMEL SAUCE:

20 g (¾ oz) butter

20 g (¾ oz) flour

250 ml (8 fl oz) milk

grated nutmeg

salt and pepper

1. Pre-heat the oven to 200°C (400°F).

2. Prepare the béchamel sauce: melt the butter with the flour in a saucepan, over low heat. Once the mix starts to froth (don't wait for it to brown), pour in the milk while whisking, over the heat, until the mix thickens. Season with salt, pepper and nutmeg.

3. Spread a generous amount of softened butter on the outside of the bread slices. Spread the béchamel on the inside.

4. Put half a slice of ham on the béchamel-coated side of 4 slices of bread. Sprinkle with some grated Gruyère. Cover with the other slices of bread (béchamel on the inside). Sprinkle the sandwiches with the remaining Gruyère and bake for 10–12 minutes.

5. Enjoy the croque-monsieur nice and hot with a side of green salad, if you like.

ENDIVES WITH HAM

—

Endives or chicories au gratin make up an autumn-winter staple.
Born in Belgium, the endive arrived in France in 1873 and never left!

—

INGREDIENTS:

8 medium-size endives

1 tablespoon thick crème fraîche

4 thick slices cooked ham

125 g (4½ oz) grated Gruyère

butter, for greasing

FOR THE BÉCHAMEL SAUCE:

50 g (1¾ oz) butter + a little for the dish

50 g (1¾ oz) flour

750 ml (25 fl oz) full-fat milk

salt and pepper

1. Core the endives through the base, steam them whole for 15 minutes, then drain.

2. Pre-heat the oven to 220°C (425°F).

3. Prepare the béchamel sauce: in a saucepan, melt the butter, add the flour and stir with a wooden spoon until the mix begins to froth (without browning).

4. Away from the heat, gradually add the milk, stirring constantly. Put the pan back on the heat and continue stirring until the mix thickens. Stir in the crème fraîche, salt and pepper.

5. Roll the ham slices around the endives, arrange them in an oven dish, greased with a little butter, and cover them in béchamel sauce. Sprinkle with grated Gruyère and bake for 20 minutes. Allow to cool for a moment before serving.

FRENCH-STYLE PETITS POIS

—

Even though they are so small, French-style petits pois are a true monument to French cuisine. Traditionally, they are prepared as a side to veal and poultry, but I can assure you that they deserve to be discovered as a dish in themselves. Your call!

—

INGREDIENTS:

1.5 kg (3 lb 5 oz) petits pois

2 nice and tight lettuce hearts

12 spring onion (scallion) bulbs

1 tablespoon caster (superfine) sugar

50 g (1¾ oz) butter at room temperature

1 bunch chervil tied with string

salt and pepper

1. Shell the petits pois. Cut the lettuce hearts into 6, lengthwise. Discard the outer skin of the spring onions and the ragged ends at the top and keep 3 cm (1¼ in) of the stalk.

2. In a large mixing bowl, put the vegetables, 1 teaspoon of salt, the sugar, 30 g (1 oz) of butter and mix well. Once the vegetables are coated in butter, salt and sugar, add the chervil. Cover and keep in the fridge for at least 30 minutes so that the chervil imparts its fragrance.

3. Pour 2 tablespoons water into a saucepan, add the vegetables and cover the pan with a deep plate filled with cold water, so as to keep the steam and prevent the petits pois from drying out.

4. Cook on low heat for 20 minutes, drain the vegetables with a slotted spoon, leaving the cooking juice in the pan.

5. Share the vegetables among the plates. Increase the heat and allow the cooking juices to evaporate, away from the heat, add the remaining 20 g (¾ oz) butter, cut into small pieces, while whisking.

6. Season with salt, pepper and drizzle the vegetables with the cooking juices. Serve immediately.

RATATOUILLE NIÇOISE

INGREDIENTS:

2 aubergines

100 ml (3½ fl oz) olive oil

4 courgettes

2 yellow onions

2 garlic cloves

1 green pepper

1 red pepper

600 g (1 lb 5 oz) ripe tomatoes

½ teaspoon sugar

1 sprig thyme

1 bay leaf

salt and pepper

1. Remove the ends of the aubergines, then dice them. Heat half the olive oil in a large sauté pan and sauté the aubergines on medium heat until they brown nicely, stirring regularly for about 15 minutes: this is the longest stage!

2. Meanwhile, dice the courgettes. Peel and finely slice the onions and cloves of garlic. Deseed the peppers and cut them into strips. Remove the stalks from the tomatoes and cut them into 4 parts.

3. Once the aubergines are cooked, put them aside in a colander.

4. Add the remaining oil into the pan and sauté the diced courgettes until soft. Add them to the aubergines. Repeat the same procedure with the peppers.

5. Cook the onions and garlic in the pan on a low heat until golden, then add the tomatoes, the remaining vegetables, the salt, pepper, sugar, thyme and bay leaf. Simmer for 30–45 minutes on a low heat, uncovered, stirring all the time. The ratatouille is ready once the vegetables are caramelised.

GRATIN DAUPHINOIS

—

Served in Gap, in the Dauphiné, at the table of the Duke of Clermont-Tonnerre, who received the gratin from the city's municipal officers, gratin dauphinois spread throughout France and shows nowhere near its age. It is still one of France's favourite side dishes.

—

INGREDIENTS:

1.2 kg (2 lb 10 oz) large potatoes (like Charlottes)

1 garlic clove

1 knob of butter for the dish

700 ml (23½ fl oz) full-fat pouring cream

salt

1. Pre-heat the oven to 150°C (300°F).

2. Peel, wash and dry the potatoes. Cut into 2-mm-thick rounds.

3. Rub a roasting dish with the peeled clove of garlic and butter it lightly.

4. Arrange a layer of potato slices in the dish, salt and cover with cream. Repeat for the rest of the potatoes.

5. Cover the dish with a sheet of greaseproof paper. Put into the oven for about 1 hour 30 minutes: the potatoes must be soft when poked with a knife.

6. Turn up the oven temperature to 200°C (400°F) 15 minutes before the end of the cooking and remove the greaseproof paper to brown the tops of the potatoes.

SERVES:
4 (24 DAUPHINE
POTATOES)

PREPARATION:
45 MINUTES

COOKING:
45 MINUTES

DAUPHINE POTATOES

INGREDIENTS:

500 g (1 lb 2 oz) floury
potatoes (like bintje)

FOR THE CHOUX PASTRY:
100 g (3½ oz) butter
200 g (7 oz) flour
4 large eggs
salt
oil, for frying

1. Peel the potatoes and cut them up. Put the potatoes in a large saucepan, fill with cold water, add salt and bring to the boil. Cook for 15–20 minutes from the moment they boil.

2. Prepare the choux pastry: pour 250 ml (8 fl oz) water into a saucepan, add 1 pinch of salt and the butter and let it melt until it boils. Remove the pan from the heat and use a wooden spoon to stir in the flour. Add the eggs, one at a time, stirring well.

3. Pre-heat the oil in a deep fryer to 170°C (340°F).

4. With a potato masher, purée the potatoes. Weigh out 500 g (1 lb 2 oz) of purée and mix it thoroughly with 500 g (1 lb 2 oz) of choux pastry.

5. Using two small spoons, form small, even pastry balls and plunge them into the deep-fryer. Cook 6 or 7 at the same time for about 10 minutes.

6. Remove the Dauphine potatoes with a slotted spoon and drain on kitchen paper. Sprinkle with salt and serve without delay.

SARLAT POTATOES

—

The name of these potatoes, sautéed in animal fat with parsley and garlic, comes from the medieval city Sarlat, in the Périgord, the 'capital' of foie gras and duck preserve.

—

INGREDIENTS:

1 kg (2 lb 4 oz) potatoes (like Belle de Fontenay, Charlotte or Amandine)

6 tablespoons goose or duck fat

3 garlic cloves

½ bunch parsley

salt

1. Peel the potatoes. Slice them into 3-mm-thick rounds with a mandoline. Wash them in a basin of cold water to remove as much starch as possible, then dry them with a clean cloth so they do not end up mushy while cooking.

2. Heat half the fat in a frying pan until it is nice and hot and add the potatoes. Cook for 3 minutes without moving them, then gently stir for 2–3 minutes, gradually adding the remaining fat. Cook for 15 minutes.

3. Sprinkle the potatoes with parsley and chopped garlic, cover and cook for a further 5 minutes. Add some salt.

4. Serve the Sarlat potatoes as a side to fillets of duck (see recipe page 126) or a nice green salad.

BOULANGÈRE POTATOES

—

Sliced very thinly, Boulangère potatoes are named after the boulanger (baker) who allowed the villagers to use the residual heat in his oven after he had baked his batch of bread to cook this lovely side dish.

—

INGREDIENTS:

1 kg (2 lb 4 oz) firm potatoes

1 kg (2 lb 4 oz) onions

2 garlic cloves

50 g (1¾ oz) butter

2 sprigs thyme

250 ml (8 fl oz) dry white wine

500 ml (17 fl oz) chicken stock

salt and pepper

1. Peel the potatoes, onions and garlic. Slice the potatoes into 2–3-mm-thick rounds with a mandoline. Slice the onions very finely.

2. Melt the butter in a frying pan. Add the onions, garlic, thyme leaves and salt, and cook covered on medium heat for 10 minutes. Once the onions are caramelised, deglaze the pan with the white wine and pour in the chicken stock. Season to taste with salt and pepper.

3. Layer the Boulangère potatoes in a roasting dish, alternating them with the onions. Finish by arranging the potatoes in concentric circles. Pour in the remaining chicken stock, add a touch more salt and bake in the oven for 45 minutes.

4. Serve straight away as a side to a leg of lamb, such as the recipe on page 122.

POMMES DARPHIN

—

Pommes Darphin are grated potato pancakes,
fried in a pan with fat – that's all. Every region has adopted them.
It is known as râpée in Lorraine, crique in Ardèche and
grumbeerekiechle in Alsace, to name but a few.

—

INGREDIENTS:

500 g (1 lb 2 oz) large
potatoes (suitable for baking
such as King Edward)

100 g (3½ oz) butter

salt and pepper

1. Peel, wash and wipe the potatoes before cutting them into julienne strips with a mandoline or the fine grater of a food processor.

2. Grease a large frying pan with butter and put in three heaps of potato strips. Add salt and pepper. Flatten them with a fork so they are nice and compact. Cook for about 8 minutes. Turn them over, add some fat if necessary and cook for a further 8 minutes or so. Add more salt and pepper.

3. Remove the patties from the pan with a slotted spoon and drain on kitchen paper. Serve them immediately with crudités or as a side to a meat dish.

FRITES

—

Frites are a French invention – even Pierre Leclerc,
the Belgian historian, says so.
As for frying them in beef fat, oil or both – to make everyone
happy – it's entirely up to you!

—

INGREDIENTS:

1 kg (2 lb 4 oz) large potatoes
(like King Edward)

2.5 kg (5 lb 8 oz) beef fat
(or 3 litres/5 lb 8 oz)
sunflower oil)

salt

1. Peel the potatoes and soak them in cool water. Rinse thoroughly. Cut them into 0.5-cm (¼-in) thick slices, lengthwise, then into 5-cm (2-in) wide rods. Rinse well in cold water to remove the starch. Drain and dry them thoroughly.

2. Heat the fat at 150°C (300°F) in a deep-fryer or pan. Immerse the fries in the oil, cooking them for 5–7 minutes, stirring every now and then. They must not brown and be soft enough once they are out of the oil. Drain on kitchen paper. This initial bath may be done in advance.

3. Immerse the potatoes in the oil a second time at 180°C (350°F). As soon as they become golden, remove using a slotted spoon, drain on kitchen paper and immediately sprinkle with generous amount of salt. Eat with your fingers!

OMELETTE

INGREDIENTS:

12 fresh eggs

50 g (1¾ oz) butter

salt and pepper

1. Prepare the omelette according to the step-by-step instructions on pages 168–169.

2. Serve immediately with a nice salad.

—

The omelette lends itself to all kinds of variations.
Here are a few famous classics that are also my favourites.

—

OMELETTE WITH BUTTON MUSHROOMS

Take 250 g (9 oz) mushrooms, remove the muddy stalks and wipe. Slice the mushrooms finely and sauté them for a few minutes in a pre-heated frying pan with a knob of butter. Put aside while you make the omelette and add them when the bottom of the omelette slides on the pan and the top is still runny.

HAM OMELETTE

Cut 200 g (7 oz) ham into 1-cm (½-in) cubes. Put aside while you make the omelette and add the mushrooms once the bottom of the omelette slides on the frying pan, before you fold it over.

CHEESE OMELETTE

Add 200 g (7 oz) grated Gruyère or Comté as soon as the bottom of the omelette slides on the frying pan and the top is still runny. Fold the omelette over, let it brown for 2 minutes and slide onto a plate.

1

Whip the eggs with a fork in a large bowl. Do not add the salt straight away.

2

Heat a non-stick frying pan. Once it is hot, add 25 g (1 oz) butter. As soon as it starts frothing, pour in half the eggs.

3

Add salt and pepper at this point and, with the back of the fork go around in a circle, drawing the omelette in from the side towards the middle, so that it does not harden immediately. Move it a little, in a circle.

4

When the bottom of the omelette slides on the frying pan and the top is still runny, fold it over and slide onto a dish. Cover with a plate to keep it warm while you follow the same method with the remaining eggs.

DESSERTS

CRÈME RENVERSÉE

INGREDIENTS:

FOR THE CARAMEL:

150 g (5½ oz) caster (superfine) sugar

50 ml (1¾ fl oz) water

FOR THE CREAM:

1 litre (34 fl oz) milk

½ vanilla pod

7 eggs

200 g (7 oz) caster (superfine) sugar

CRÈME RENVERSÉE, CRÈME BRÛLÉE OR CRÈME CARAMEL?

Crème renversée always contains caramel and it is removed from its mould by being turned upside down.

Crème brûlée, on the other hand, does not have any.

Crème caramel is made only with egg yolks, which renders it more fragile, which is why it is eaten straight from its container, leaving the caramel at the bottom.

1. Prepare the caramel: heat the sugar and water in a saucepan on medium heat without stirring. As soon as the caramel turns a dark blonde remove the pan from the heat. Pour into an ovenproof dish so it is about 2–3 mm thick and allow to cool at room temperature.

2. Pre-heat the oven to 160°C (325°F).

3. Add the milk to a saucepan. Split the vanilla pod in half, scrape the seeds into the pan and throw in the pod too. Put over a medium heat. As soon as it comes to the boil, turn off the ring and remove the vanilla pod. Put over medium heat.

4. Mix the eggs and sugar in a bowl. Gradually add the hot milk while constantly whisking. Pour the mix through a fine sieve into a bowl and skim away any skin that forms on the surface.

5. Pour the mix into the dish with the caramel. Half-fill a rimmed baking tray with water and carefully place the dish with the caramel inside. Place into the oven and cook for 50 minutes. Check how it is cooking with the tip of a knife (it must come back out clean when you prick the cream).

6. Allow to cool out of the oven and chill in the fridge for 4 hours. To remove it from the mould, run the blade of a small knife against the inner rim of the dish and turn the cream upside down on a large flat plate. Serve immediately.

RICE PUDDING

—

Smooth, creamy and round, here is a child's dessert that brings everyone to gather around the table. Once you get the hang of making it, do try livening it up with cinnamon, star anise or tonka beans, depending on your mood.

—

INGREDIENTS:

1 litre (34 fl oz)
full-fat milk

1 vanilla pod

40 g (1½ oz) caster (superfine)
sugar

150 g (5½ oz) short-grain rice

1. Pour the milk into a saucepan.

2. Split the vanilla pod in two, scrape the seeds into the milk and bring to the boil.

3. Add the sugar and rice, and simmer over a low heat for 40 minutes, stirring occasionally.

4. Serve the rice pudding warm or cold.

STRAWBERRY CHARLOTTE

—

*The Charlotte is originally a cousin of the sponge pudding.
Antonin Carême, once a pastry chef for the English Royal Family,
returned to France with a version that did not require baking, with a
sponge finger base and Bavarian cream. The Charlotte has become lighter
over the centuries. Bavarian cream, rich in eggs and cream,
has made way to fromage blanc mixed with gelatine.*

—

INGREDIENTS:

4 sheets of gelatine

750 g (1 lb 10 oz) strawberries
+ extra 10 for the decoration

300 g (10½ oz) fromage blanc
with 20% fat (drained well)

3 egg whites

50 g (1¾ oz) caster (superfine)
sugar

12–15 sponge fingers

EQUIPMENT:

1 charlotte mould or
1 pudding basin
(18 cm (7 in) diameter)

1. Soak the gelatine in cold water.

2. Rinse the strawberries, hull them and blend them to obtain
   a coulis. Keep one-third aside to soak the biscuits.

3. Wring the gelatine and melt it in a ladle of strawberry
   coulis. Whip the well-drained fromage blanc with the
   remaining coulis and melted gelatine.

4. Whip up the egg whites to soft peaks, adding the sugar to
   make them more compact, then gently fold them into the
   mix with a spatula.

5. Line a Charlotte mould or pudding basin with cling film
   (plastic wrap). Arrange on it the sponge fingers soaked
   in coulis. Pour the strawberry mousse in the middle and
   refrigerate the Charlotte for at least 3 hours.

6. Remove the Charlotte from the mould, decorate with the
   remaining strawberries and serve chilled.

CLAFOUTIS

INGREDIENTS:

100 g (3½ oz) caster
(superfine) sugar + a little for
the dish and when serving

3 eggs

100 g (3½ oz) flour

1 pinch salt

300 ml (10 fl oz) full-fat milk

500 g (1 lb 2 oz) large cherries
(like Royal Anne)

butter, for the dish

1. Whisk the sugar and eggs in a mixing bowl, then add the flour and salt.

2. Add the milk a little at a time, always whisking to get a smooth batter.

3. Pre-heat the oven to 180°C (350°F).

4. Arrange the cherries (not stoned) in a greased, deep dish dusted with sugar and pour the batter over them. Bake the clafoutis for about 40 minutes.

5. Once it has become golden and slightly quivering in the middle, take it out of the oven and dust it with a little sugar. Allow to cool before serving.

A CHERRY IN THE CAKE

I like to prick the cherries with the tip of a knife before pouring the batter: doing this adds colour and fragrance during baking. A drop of kirsch can intensify the aroma.

BANANAS FLAMBÉ

INGREDIENTS:

4 bananas

40 g (1½ oz) butter

3 tablespoons brown sugar

2 tablespoons dark rum

juice of 1 lime

1. Peel the bananas and cut them in half, lengthwise.

2. Heat the butter in a large frying pan. Add the bananas and quickly brown them on both sides. Dust with the sugar and add the rum, then ignite.

3. Use a spoon to baste the bananas with the flaming liquid until the flame goes out. Divide the bananas among 4 plates, with the caramelised juice, drizzle with lime juice and serve immediately.

ŒUFS À LA NEIGE

INGREDIENTS:

5 eggs

700 ml (24 fl oz) milk

1 vanilla pod

70 g (2½ oz) caster (superfine) sugar

1 pinch of salt

1. Separate the egg whites from the yolks.

2. Prepare the custard: bring the milk to the boil in a pan with the vanilla pod, split in two lengthwise and seeds scraped into the pan. Blanch the egg yolks with 60 g (2 oz) sugar, pour the boiling milk over them and put the mix back on a low heat so it thickens, stirring constantly (without letting the cream boil) with a wooden spatula. Once the cream starts to coat the spatula remove from the heat, take out the vanilla pod and allow to cool.

3. Prepare the œufs à la neige according to the step-by-step instructions on pages 186–187.

4. Serve the custard, chilled, in a deep bowl, garnished with the oeufs à la neige.

FLOATING ISLAND OR ŒUFS À LA NEIGE?

Although the same basic ingredients are used in these dishes, the egg whites are cooked differently in œufs à la neige. In floating islands the egg whites are whipped with sugar then cooked in ramekins on a double boiler in the oven. They are then turned out onto the custard.

1

Whip the egg whites on slow speed. Once they start frothing, add sugar to firm them up.

2

Keep whipping until you obtain soft peaks.

3

Heat 2 litres (68 fl oz) of water and maintain it at 85°C/185°F (if you don't have a cooking thermometer, keep it simmering gently). Lay small ladles of whipped egg whites on the water and poach them for 5–7 minutes on one side, then 2–3 minutes on the other.

4

Drain on a clean, dry cloth.

FLAN PÂTISSIER

—

This dessert boasts different names throughout the world: pasteis de nata in Portugal, custard tart in the United Kingdom… But let me be biased and say there is no match for French-style Flan pâtissier!

—

INGREDIENTS:

1 sweet tart crust
(page 237)

FOR THE FILLING:

1 litre (34 fl oz)
full-fat milk

1 vanilla pod

250 g (9 oz) caster (superfine)
sugar

2 eggs + 4 egg yolks

100 g (3½ oz) cornflour
(cornstarch)

200 ml (7 fl oz) full-fat
pouring cream

EQUIPMENT:

1 mould,
22 cm (8¾ in) diameter and
4.5 cm (1¾ in) deep

1. Prepare the sweet tart crust following the recipe on page 237.

2. Pre-heat the oven to 180°C (350°F).

3. Prepare the filling: in a large saucepan, bring to the boil the milk with the vanilla pod, split in two and seeds scraped into the pan, as well as 50 g (1¾ oz) of sugar.

4. In a large mixing bowl, whip the eggs with the yolks, cornflour and remaining sugar until the mix whitens. Pour the hot milk over it, stirring constantly, followed by the cream.

5. Pour everything into a saucepan and put over a low heat, whisking non-stop until the cream thickens and starts to boil. Remove the vanilla pod and allow to cool away from the heat.

6. Meanwhile, roll out the pastry on a worktop and line a greased mould with it. Pour the filling into it and smooth the surface.

7. Bake for 50 minutes: the flan should brown nicely.

8. Remove from the oven and allow to cool down then refrigerate for at least 6 hours.

SERVES:
4-6

PREPARATION:
35 MINUTES

COOKING:
35-40 MINUTES

CHILLING:
2 HOURS MINIMUM

LEMON TART

INGREDIENTS:

**1 sweet tart crust
(page 237)**

FOR THE LEMON FILLING:

3 eggs

**120 g (4½ oz) caster
(superfine) sugar**

**10 g (½ oz) cornflour
(cornstarch)**

3 unwaxed lemons

**80 g (2¾ oz) butter at room
temperature, cut into chunks**

EQUIPMENT:

**1 x 22 cm- (8¾ in-) diameter
non-stick or greased mould**

1. Prepare the sweet tart crust following the recipe on page 237.

2. Pre-heat the oven to 180°C (350°F).

3. Roll out the dough so it is 3 cm (1¼ in) thick on a lightly floured worktop and put it in the mould. Cover with greaseproof paper and fill with baking beans. Bake for 15 minutes, remove the beans then bake for a further 15 minutes.

4. Prepare the lemon filling. In a mixing bowl, whip the eggs and sugar. Add the cornflour and stir.

5. Finely grate the zest of lemon into a saucepan and squeeze in the juice of 3 lemons. Place over a low heat, pour in the egg mixture, whisking quickly. Cook until the mixture thickens, whisking all the time.

6. In a mixing bowl, strain the mix and add the butter. Blend with a hand blender until you have a very smooth cream. If you do not have a hand blender, pour the mix through a sieve.

TARTE BOURDALOUE (FRENCH PEAR TART)

—

When a pastry is named after a street in Paris, we have Tarte Bourdaloue. This almondy pear tart was created in the Paris 9th Arrondissement in around 1860, most probably by the pastry chef Fasquelle. It's always popular.

—

INGREDIENTS:
1 sweet tart crust
(page 237)

FOR THE PEARS
IN SYRUP:

500 g (1 lb 2 oz) caster
(superfine) sugar

juice of 1 lemon

4 William pears

1–2 tablespoons flaked
almonds (optional)

FOR THE ALMOND PASTE:

100 g (3½ oz) softened butter

100 g (3½ oz) caster
(superfine) sugar

2 whole eggs

100 g (3½ oz) ground almonds

1 teaspoon rum or bitter
almond aroma (optional)

EQUIPMENT:

1 x 28 cm- (11 in-) diameter
non-stick or greased mould

1. Prepare the sweet tart crust following the recipe on page 237.

2. Prepare the pears in syrup: bring 1.5 litres (51 fl oz) of water to the boil with the sugar and lemon juice and cook for 5 minutes. Core the pears from the bottom and peel them. Immerse them in the syrup and simmer gently for 10–15 minutes. Drain.

3. Line the mould with the dough and refrigerate.

4. Prepare the almond paste: beat together the butter and sugar, then whisk in the eggs, one at a time, until you obtain a smooth mixture. Add the ground almonds and rum or bitter almond aroma if you wish.

5. Pre-heat the oven to 180°C (350°F).

6. Cut the pears in two, lengthwise. Spread the almond paste over the base of the tart. Arrange the pears on top, sprinkle with almond flakes and bake for 35 minutes. Serve preferably warm.

APPLE TARTLETS

INGREDIENTS:

4 x 100 g (3½ oz) lots of homemade puff pastry (page 237) or 400 g (14 oz) pure butter puff pastry

8 apples (like King of the Pippins)

100 g (3½ oz) butter

100 g (3½ oz) caster (superfine) sugar

4 pinches ground cinnamon

1. Prepare the puff pastry following the recipe on page 237.

2. Pre-heat the oven to 210°C (410°F).

3. Roll out 4 puff pastry circles, 16–18 cm (6¼–7 in) in diameter, on a floured worktop. Prick them with a fork and transfer them to a baking tray or oven drip tray.

4. Peel and core the apples. Cut them in half, lengthwise, and slice finely.

5. Arrange them in a concentric circle on the pastry circles. Sprinkle with 25 g (1 oz) of finely diced butter per tartlet, the dust with 25 g (1 oz) of sugar per tartlet and 1 pinch of cinnamon. Bake for 15–20 minutes.

6. Allow to cool. Serve.

SERVES:
6

PREPARATION:
20 MINUTES

COOKING:
35 MINUTES

RESTING:
10 MINUTES

TARTE TATIN

INGREDIENTS:

**400 g (14 oz) homemade
sweet shortcrust pastry
(page 236)**

200 ml (7 fl oz) double cream

FOR THE CARAMELISED
APPLES:

**1.7 kg (3 lb 12 oz) sweet apples
(like Golden Delicious)**

100 g (3½ oz) butter

**150 g (5½ oz) caster
(superfine) sugar**

EQUIPMENT:

**24 cm (9½ in) springform
cake tin also suitable for hobs
or a cast-iron pan**

1. Prepare the shortcrust pastry following the recipe on page 236.

2. Prepare the caramelised apples: peel and core the apples, then cut them in four, lengthwise.

3. Melt the butter and sugar in the springform cake tin on a low heat. Away from the heat, arrange the apple quarters in the tin nice and compactly.

4. Put back on the hob. As soon as caramel forms under the apples, remove the tin from the heat and allow to cool for 10 minutes.

5. Pre-heat the oven to 200°C (400°F).

6. Put the pastry on a floured worktop and form a circle that is slightly wider than the diameter of the cake tin, then prick with a fork. Cover with the apples then tuck in the edges of the pastry inside the cake tin. Bake in the middle of the oven for 20 minutes.

7. Once baked, cover the tin with a large dish and turn the tart out. Serve warm with double cream.

AN INVENTION BY THE TATIN SISTERS?

The story of the Tatin sisters and their accidentally created tart is a legend: upside puddings already existed even before them. However, it was the sisters who, in 20th century Lamotte-Beuvron made this dessert famous in their native Sologne as they had the stroke of genius to caramelise the apples. Allegedly, their gardener purloined the recipe from the chef at the Parisian restaurant Maxim's, thereby spreading the reputation of this tart.

MILLEFEUILLE

—

Although La Varenne published the first recipe for millefeuille in Le Cuisinier françois, this pastry lay forgotten for over two centuries before being made popular by the pastry chef Sergent in 1867.

—

INGREDIENTS:

500 g (1 lb 2 oz) homemade puff pastry (page 237) or 3 sheets of pure butter puff pastry ready to unroll

250 ml (8 fl oz) chilled single cream

100 g (3½ oz) icing (powdered) sugar

FOR THE CRÈME PÂTISSIÈRE
(FOR 1.2 KG/2 LB 10 OZ):

1 litre (34 fl oz) milk

1 vanilla pod

6 egg yolks

250 g (9 oz) caster (superfine) sugar

100 g (3½ oz) flour

1. Prepare the puff pastry following the recipe on page 237. Pre-heat the oven to 200°C (400°F).

2. With a rolling pin, spread the pastry and cut out three 24 x 9 cm (9½ x 3½ in) squares. Prick them with a fork and bake for 20 minutes on a sheet lined with baking paper.

3. Meanwhile, prepare the crème pâtissière: in a saucepan, boil the milk and the vanilla pod, split in two and seeds scraped into the pan. Allow to infuse for 10 minutes away from the heat, then remove the pod.

4. Whisk the egg yolks and sugar in a mixing bowl until the mixture has whitened. Add the flour and stir. Pour in the cooled milk mixture in two parts, whisking. Pour the mixture into the pan and cook on a low heat, continuously stirring, until thickened. Allow to cool.

5. Whip the cream. Stir the crème pâtissière gently then fold it into the whipped cream. Allow to firm up in the fridge for 1 hour.

6. Spread a 1.5–2-cm (½–¾ in) layer of cream on the first puff pastry rectangle. Place the second square of puff pastry on top and repeat, ending with the most regular rectangle of puff pastry on top. Spread over the remaining area, on the sides, and smooth with a spatula.

7. Using a bread knife, cut the millefeuille into even portions and dust with icing sugar. Serve on the same day it is made.

RUM BABA

—

The rum baba is a monument to French pâtisserie. When in large format, it is called a savarin, from the name of the ring-shaped mould. Garnished with whipped cream in the centre, this is the XXL, simplified version of the individual baba.

—

INGREDIENTS:

FOR THE BABA:

80 ml (2½ fl oz) milk

12 g (½ oz) fresh yeast

250 g (9 oz) flour

50 g (1¾ oz) caster (superfine) sugar

1 flat teaspoon salt

2 eggs

80 g (2¾ oz) softened butter + a little for greasing the mould

FOR THE WHIPPED CREAM:

400 ml (14 fl oz) pouring cream with 35 % fat

1 vanilla pod

30 g (1 oz) icing (powdered) sugar

FOR THE SYRUP:

50 g (1¾ oz) caster (superfine) sugar

zest of 1 orange

100 ml (3½ fl oz) good-quality dark or amber rum

EQUIPMENT:

24 cm (9½ in) diameter savarin mould

1. In a saucepan, slightly warm the milk over a low heat. Transfer it to a bowl, add the yeast and stir to dissolve it.

2. In a food mixer or the tub of a food processor fitted with a flat beater, mix the flour, sugar and salt. Make a well in the centre. Beat the eggs and add, along with the milk and yeast mixture, then gradually stir in the flour with a wooden spoon until you have a smooth dough. It must be soft and homogenous. Little by little, incorporate the butter, cut into pieces. Cover with a damp cloth and allow the dough to prove for 30 minutes in a warm place.

3. Prepare the whipped cream: split the vanilla pod in two, lengthwise, and scrape out the seeds with a small knife, then whip the cream and vanilla seeds with a whisk, gradually incorporating the icing sugar. Put the cream into the fridge.

4. Pre–heat the oven to 200°C (400°F).

5. Grease the savarin mould and pour the dough into it. Bake for 25–30 minutes, then let it cool down.

6. Prepare the syrup: add the water and the sugar to a saucepan and bring to the boil. Allow to simmer for 5 minutes. Remove from the heat, add the orange zest and rum.

7. Turn out the baba on a cooling rack and soak it in the syrup a little at a time. Repeat until you have used up the syrup, then transfer the baba to a serving dish. Fill a fluted piping bag with the whipped cream and pipe into each baba.

8. Serve immediately.

BABA'S BABA

Towards the end of his life, the king of Poland, Stanislas Leszczynski (1677–1766), who had become the Duke of Lorraine, had gum problems. In the kitchen, a crafty person came up with the idea of soaking a raisin brioche in Malaga wine. In the middle of the 19th century, the wine was replaced with rum, and then the baba was filled with crème pâtissière or whipped cream.

SABAYON WITH SOFT FRUIT

INGREDIENTS:

250 g (9 oz) strawberries

125 g (4½ oz) raspberries

125 g (4½ oz) blueberries or
blackcurrants

4 egg yolks

80 g (2¾ oz) caster
(superfine) sugar

100 g (3½ oz) pouring cream
with minimum 30% fat
(chilled)

1. Rinse the fruit and hull the strawberries. Cut them up and put them into oven-proof ramekins. Divide the remaining fruit and put it on top.

2. In a heat-proof mixing bowl, mix the egg yolks and sugar, then cook them on a double boiler, whisking so as to incorporate some air, until you have a creamy foam: the mixture must double in volume.

3. Keep whisking away from the heat until the mixture cools down. Whip the cream with a food mixer and add it to the filling.

4. Cover the fruit with a thin layer of sabayon and put under the oven grill for 5 minutes so it browns a little. Serve immediately.

MOELLEUX AU CHOCOLAT

—

This now classic dessert is a variation on the famous coulant au chocolat created by chef Michel Bras. In its early version, the biscuit conceals a frozen chocolate core that turns liquid after baking.

—

INGREDIENTS:

250 g (9 oz) dark chocolate, minimum 75 % cocoa

120 g (4½ oz) butter + a little for greasing

8 eggs

150 g (5½ oz) caster (superfine) sugar

120 g (4½ oz) sifted flour + a little for the mould

EQUIPMENT:

1 round cake tin, 22 cm (8¾ in) diameter

1. Pre-heat the oven to 180°C (350°F).

2. Melt the chocolate and butter, cut up, on a double boiler.

3. Grease the tin and dust it with flour. Separate the egg whites from the yolks. With a food mixer, whip the egg whites on a slow setting, gradually adding the sugar to obtain a meringue. Then add the yolks one at a time.

4. Gently fold in the melted chocolate and butter, then the flour.

5. Pour the mixture into the tin and bake for 25 minutes.

6. Allow the cake to cool, turn it out of the tin and serve with a scoop of good-quality (or homemade, see recipe page 240) vanilla ice cream or custard.

CHOCOLATE SOUFFLÉ

INGREDIENTS:

20 g (¾ oz) **melted butter**

100 g (3½ oz) **golden cane
sugar**

300 g (10½ oz) **dark chocolate,
minimum 70% cocoa**

1 **pinch of salt**

6 **egg whites**

4 **egg yolks**

400 ml (14 fl oz) **full-fat milk**

25 g (1 oz) **cornflour
(cornstarch)**

1 teaspoon **icing (powdered)
sugar**

EQUIPMENT:

1 **tall cake tin,
20 cm (8 in) diameter**

1. Pre-heat the oven to 160°C (325°F).

2. Grease the tin from the bottom up with a brush. Dust
   the inside with 20 g (¾ oz) of sugar and put in the fridge.

3. In a large mixing bowl, melt the chocolate and salt on a
   double boiler.

4. Whip the egg whites and 40 g (1½ oz) of sugar briskly.
   Once the mixture is firm, add the remaining sugar.

5. In a saucepan, heat the milk and cornflour, stirring
   constantly. As soon as the mixture thickens, pour it on the
   melted chocolate and stir. Add the egg yolks and stir again.
   Fold in one third of the egg whites with a whisk, then the
   rest with a spatula.

6. Pour the mixture into the tin and bake for 35 minutes.

7. Dust with icing sugar and serve immediately.

CHOCOLATE MOUSSE

INGREDIENTS:

250 g (9 oz) dark chocolate, minimum 66 % cocoa

20 g (¾ oz) butter

4 eggs + 2 egg whites

25 g (1 oz) caster (superfine) sugar

1. Melt the chocolate and butter on a double boiler.

2. Separate the egg whites from the yolks. Beat the yolks with half the sugar until white. Stir in the melted chocolate.

3. Whip up the egg whites, gradually adding the remaining sugar. Gently fold this mixture into the melted, still warm chocolate with a spatula.

4. Pour the mousse into coupes and refrigerate for 2–24 hours.

5. Serve the mousse with *langues-de-chat* biscuits, for example.

THE MOUSSE SCHOOL

There are two schools of thoughts where mousse is concerned. One includes egg whites, whipped with sugar and called 'French-style meringues'. The other style opts for whipped cream. Some people actually make both! I prefer the first, lighter version.

SERVES:
4 (2-3 PANCAKES PER
PERSON)

PREPARATION:
20 MINUTES

COOKING:
5 MINUTES (IN ADDITION
TO COOKING THE
PANCAKES)

CRÊPES SUZETTE

—

Auguste Escoffier did not flambé them but would add mandarine and soak them in curaçao. He allegedly created this dessert at the end of the 19th century to pay tribute to actress Suzanne Reichenberg. Here's to a blazing good party!

—

INGREDIENTS:

FOR THE PANCAKE
BATTER:

50 g (1¾ oz) butter
+ a little for greasing while
frying the pancakes

250 g (9 oz) flour

30 g (1 oz) caster (superfine)
sugar

1 pinch of salt

3 eggs

500 ml (17 fl oz) milk

FOR THE SUZETTE
SAUCE:

1 unwaxed lemon

2 unwaxed oranges

2 tablespoons Grand Marnier

50 g (1¾ oz) caster (superfine)
sugar

20 g (¾ oz) butter

50 ml (¾ fl oz/2 tablespoons)
cognac

1. Prepare the pancake batter: melt the butter in a saucepan without letting it brown. Put the flour, sugar and salt into a mixing bowl. Form a well in the middle, and add the eggs. Stir. Add the milk, a little at a time, to blend it with the dough. Add the melted butter.

2. Melt a little butter in a frying pan and fry the pancakes, one at a time, until slightly golden. Set aside.

3. Prepare the Suzette sauce: slice the lemon zest and the zest of 1 orange into fine strips. Squeeze the 2 oranges and mix their juice with the Grand Marnier.

4. Heat the sugar and orange juice mixture in a frying pan. Once the mixture turns into a thick syrup, add the butter. Stir with a wooden spatula and soak the pancakes in the syrup on both sides by quickly immersing them in it. Fold them into triangles and arrange on plates.

5. Heat the cognac in the frying pan, flambé it and pour it immediately over the pancakes. Serve hot.

MAKES
20 LARGE
MADELEINE CAKES
(OR 40 SMALL
ONES)

PREPARATION:
15 MINUTES

FREEZING
(OPTIONAL):
2 HOURS

COOKING:
9-10 MINUTES

MADELEINES

—

Like the crêpe Suzette (page 218), the origin of the madeleine is a moot point. One thing is certain: it was born in Lorraine, like me! In Commercy, to be precise.

—

INGREDIENTS:

200 g (7 oz) caster (superfine) sugar

4 eggs

70 g (2½ oz) full-fat milk

250 g (9 oz) flour

1 sachet baking powder (11 g/½ oz)

160 g (5½ oz) butter

EQUIPMENT:

1 madeleine mould baking tray

1. Pre-heat the oven to 180°C (350°F).

2. In a mixing bowl, whisk together the eggs and the sugar. Pour in the milk, then sift in the flour and baking powder. Melt the butter, let it cool and stir it into the mixture.

3. Grease the madeleine tin with butter. Dollop a spoonful of batter into the centre of each mould and tap so it gets distributed evenly.

4. To obtain nice ridges, you can let the madeleines rest for 2 hours in the freezer before baking them for 7–10 minutes.

MAKES
15-20 DOUGHNUTS

PREPARATION:
20 MINUTES

CHILLING:
4-5 HOURS

COOKING:
5 MINUTES

BUGNES

—

Traditionally made on Shrove Tuesday in the Lyon region, bugnes are small doughnuts enjoyed since Ancient Rome. They are called chichis frégis in Provence and merveilles in South-Western France.

—

INGREDIENTS:

250 g (9 oz) flour

50 g (1¾ oz) softened butter

30 g (1 oz) caster (superfine) sugar

1 pinch of salt

2 large eggs

juice of ½ orange

1 teaspoon dark rum

icing (powdered) sugar

zest of 1 lime

sunflower oil, for frying

1. Sift the flour in a large mixing bowl. Add the butter, sugar, salt, beaten eggs, orange juice and rum. Mix and knead for 15–20 minutes. Form the dough into a ball and let it rest in the fridge for 4–5 hours.

2. Roll the dough so it is 5 mm (½ in) thick. Cut it into 10 × 4 cm (4 x ½ in) strips. Slit the middle of the strip and thread one end of the dough to form a kind of knot.

3. Deep-fry the *bugnes* in oil heated to 180°C (350°F). Drain them on kitchen paper. Dust with icing sugar and grate with lime zest before serving.

PEACH MELBA

—

Auguste Escoffier – him again – created this dessert in 1894 for Nellie Melba, an Australian singer. He is said to have served poached peaches resting between the wings of a swan sculpted from ice, covered with raspberry purée. Here is the modern version.

—

INGREDIENTS:

4 yellow peaches
(ripe but firm)

150 g (5½ oz) caster
(superfine) sugar

juice of 1 lemon

1 vanilla pod

250–300 g (9–10½ oz)
raspberries

80 g (2¾ oz) icing (powdered)
sugar

500 ml (17 fl oz) good-quality
vanilla ice cream (or see
recipe on page 240)

1. Immerse the peaches in hot water for 30 seconds so they are easier to peel. Cut them in half, and remove the stones.

2. Place 700 ml (24 fl oz) of water and icing sugar, juice of half a lemon and vanilla pod, split in half and seeds scraped, into a saucepan and bring to the boil. Simmer for 10 minutes.

3. Turn down the heat, add the peach halves, cook for 8–10 minutes, then allow to cool in the syrup.

4. In a bowl, crush the raspberries with a fork. Add the icing sugar and the rest of the lemon juice. Stir and strain through a cheesecloth (muslin) to obtain a smooth coulis.

5. Place one half of a peach in every coupe. Add a scoop of vanilla ice cream and cover with the other half peach. Cover with raspberry coulis and serve straight away.

PEARS BELLE-HÉLÈNE

—

Invented in Paris in 1864 in honour of the singer Hortense Schneider, who performed Offenbach's operetta La Belle Hélène, this dessert with poached pears is a delight for the taste buds.

—

INGREDIENTS:

100 g (3½ oz) caster (superfine) sugar

1 vanilla pod

4 seasonal pears

150 g (5½ oz) dark chocolate, minimum 64% cocoa

150 ml (5 fl oz) pouring crème fraîche with 30% fat, at room temperature

500 ml (17 fl oz) good-quality vanilla ice cream (or see recipe on page 240)

20 g (¾ oz) toasted almond flakes (optional)

1. In a saucepan, bring 500 ml (17 fl oz) of water to the boil for 5 minutes with the sugar and the vanilla pod, split in two and scraped.

2. Peel the pears, leaving the stalks intact and core them from the bottom. Add them to the syrup and poach for 15–20 minutes, simmering. Drain them with a slotted spoon and set aside on a dish.

3. Melt the chocolate on a double boiler and add the crème fraîche. Stir.

4. Put the pears into deep plates. Coat them in chocolate and add a scoop of vanilla ice cream. Sprinkle with toasted almond flakes.

CHOCOLATE PROFITEROLES

INGREDIENTS:

125 g (4½ oz) dark chocolate

200 ml (7 fl oz) good-quality vanilla ice cream (or see recipe on page 240)

FOR THE PUFFS:

1 pinch of salt

75 g (2½ oz) butter

1 tablespoon caster (superfine) sugar

125 g (4½ oz) flour

3 large eggs

1. Pre-heat the oven to 180°C (350°F).

2. Prepare the puffs: in a saucepan, pour 200 ml (7 fl oz) of water, add the salt, butter and sugar. Bring to the boil, then stir in the flour.

3. Stir well with a spatula for about 5 minutes over low heat until the dough comes away from the sides of a pan and forms a ball. Away from the heat, add the eggs, one at a time, stirring the dough briskly as you add them.

4. Form a puff with the help of a piping bag or a spoon (4–5 puffs per person). Bake for 15–20 minutes without opening the oven door while they are baking. Take the puffs out and let cool.

5. Cut the puffs in half, sidewise, and fill with a scoop of vanilla ice cream. Melt the chocolate on a double boiler and immediately coat the puffs in it. Serve immediately.

HOMEMADE

MAKES:
1 LITRE (34 FL OZ)
WHITE VEAL STOCK

PREPARATION:
30 MINS

COOKING:
2 HOURS 30 MINUTES
-3 HOURS

WHITE STOCK

—

White stock makes a good base for soups, broths for risottos, etc.

—

INGREDIENTS:

1 kg (2 lb 4 oz) veal bones
(knuckles, shank, feet, lean
trimmings)

2 carrots

2 onions

2 cloves

1 bouquet garni (thyme, bay
leaf and flat-leaf parsley tied
with a strip of leek green)

1 garlic clove

1. Chop the bones with a small cleaver or a heavy knife and put them into a thick-bottomed casserole (Dutch oven). Moisten with cold water and bring to the boil. Skim regularly.

2. Peel the vegetables and cut the carrots into chunks. Stick the cloves into the onion and put them into the casserole with bouquet garni and the garlic. Simmer for 2 hours 20 minutes–3 hours, skimming regularly.

3. Pour the stock through a fine sieve into a container, allow to cool and freeze.

MAKES:
1 LITRE (34 FL OZ)
BROWN VEAL STOCK

PREPARATION:
30 MINUTES

COOKING:
3-4 HOURS

BROWN STOCK

INGREDIENTS:

1 kg (2 lb 4 oz) veal bones
(knuckles, shank, feet, lean
trimmings)

2 carrots

2 onions

1 garlic bulb

200 g (7 oz) tomatoes (or
20 g/¾ oz tomato purée)

1 bouquet garni (thyme, bay
leaf and flat-leaf parsley tied
with a strip of leek green)

1 large pinch of salt

1. Chop the bones with a small cleaver or a heavy knife and put on a baking tray. Brown them in the oven at 200°C (400°F) for 20–30 minutes turning them over regularly.

2. Peel the carrots and the onions, cut them into large cubes and add them to the tray, then bake everything for a further 10 minutes.

3. Put the bones and vegetables into a casserole (Dutch oven). Deglaze the baking tray with cold water and add the cooking juice over the bones. Crush the garlic bulb and chop the tomatoes. Put them both into the casserole with the garlic and the bouquet garni. Add salt. Moisten with cold water and simmer gently for 3–4 hours, skimming regularly. Add a little water if necessary.

4. Pour the stock through a fine sieve into a container. Allow to cool, remove the fat with a slotted spoon.

MAKES:
1 BALL OF DOUGH

PREPARATION:
15 MINUTES

RESTING:
2 HOURS

PIZZA DOUGH

INGREDIENTS:

10 g (¼ oz) fresh
baker's yeast

1 teaspoon sugar

350 g (12½ oz) flour
type T65

1 teaspoon salt

3 tablespoons
olive oil

1. Dilute the yeast and sugar in 50 ml (1¾ fl oz) warm water.

2. Pour the flour in a mixing bowl and form a well. Gradually pour in the diluted yeast and sugar, the salt and 150–200 ml (5–7 fl oz) of warm water, then mix and knead to form a dough. Gradually incorporate the olive oil: the dough must be very smooth.

3. Form into a ball and transfer to a mixing bowl, cover with a clean cloth and let rest for 2 hours at room temperature.

4. Flatten the dough with your hands on a floured worktop to expel the air then fold it. Form one or two balls, wrap them in cling film (plastic wrap) and keep in the fridge until you need them.

MAKES:
1 QUICHE FOR
6-8 PEOPLE

PREPARATION:
10 MINUTES

REFRIGERATE:
2 HOURS

SAVOURY SHORTCRUST PASTRY

INGREDIENTS:

200 g (7 oz) flour

1 flat teaspoon salt

100 g (3½ oz) butter,
cut into pieces

1. Form a well with the flour and salt on a worktop. Put the butter in the centre. Mix with your fingertips, gradually incorporating the flour and adding 2–3 tablespoons of cold water until the dough is homogenous. Knead until it is smooth and does not stick. Roll it into a ball, wrap in cling film (plastic wrap) and leave to rest for 1 hour in a cool place. The dough is now ready to use.

To make sweet shortcrust pastry, simply add 60 g (2 oz) icing (powdered) sugar to your mixture after pouring in the cold water and knead until you have obtained a homogenous dough.

MAKES:
2 BALLS OF DOUGH

PREPARATION:
15 MINUTES

RESTING:
1-2 HOURS

PUFF PASTRY

INGREDIENTS:

500 g (1 lb 2 oz) flour

10 g (½ oz) salt

75 g (2½ oz) butter

**375 g (13 oz) extra dry
butter with minimum
83% fat**

1. Prepare the dough: sift the flour into the bowl of the mixer or fitted food processor, fitted with a hook. Incorporate the salt, 250 ml (8 fl oz) of water and knead the dough as little as possible. Add the melted, cooled butter and knead lightly. Form a ball, cut a 1 cm- (½ in-) deep cross into it and leave to rest for 20–30 minutes in the fridge.

2. Roll the dough out with a rolling pin, soften the extra-dry butter between two sheets of greaseproof paper so it is the same consistency as the dough. Form an even rectangle, about 1 cm (½ in) thick.

3. Roll out the dough so it is three times longer than the square of butter and put the latter in the middle. Fold the edges over the butter. With a rolling pin, spread the ball of dough to obtain a rectangle that is three times longer than it is wide.

4. Turn the pastry the first time: fold one third towards the middle, then the last third over the other two. Turn a second time: turn the ball of dough a quarter of a turn so the opening to the folding is on the right. Roll out the pastry into a rectangle three times longer than it is wide. Once again, place the fold on the right, so you have a point of reference for the next turn. Leave the dough ball to rest in the fridge for 20–30 minutes.

5. Give the dough ball two more turns, as per before. Leave to rest for 20–30 minutes, then give it two final turns. The dough is now ready to use.

MAKES:
1 TART FOR 8 PEOPLE

PREPARATION:
15 MINUTES

REFRIGERATION:
1 HOUR

SWEET TART CRUST

INGREDIENTS:

120 g (4½ oz) butter

**80 g (2¾ oz) icing
(powdered) sugar**

1 egg

250 g (9 oz) flour

1. Mix the butter, diced, and the icing sugar with a wooden spoon. Incorporate the egg, beaten, then add the flour until you have obtained a homogeneous dough. Wrap in cling film (plastic wrap) and keep in a cool place for at least 1 hour.

MAKES:
1 LITRE

PREPARATION:
20 MINUTES

REFRIGERATE:
12 HOURS

FREEZE:
MINIMUM 6 HOURS

VANILLA ICE CREAM

INGREDIENTS:

250 ml (8 fl oz) full-fat milk

250 ml (8 fl oz) pouring cream
with minimum 30% fat

1 vanilla pod

6 egg yolks

150 g (5 oz) caster (superfine)
sugar

EQUIPMENT:

ice cream maker

1. Prepare the custard: put the milk into a saucepan together with the cream and the vanilla pod, split in two and scraped, including the seeds. Bring to the boil.

2. Meanwhile, whisk the egg yolks and sugar.

3. Remove the vanilla pod from the milk, then pour over the beaten eggs after removing the vanilla pod, stirring well. Transfer everything to a saucepan on a low heat.

4. Stir constantly, forming a figure of eight with a spatula. Once the cream coats the spoon (or has reached 85°C/185°C), turn off the heat. Pour the cream into a mixing bowl, cover with cling film (plastic wrap) so it touches the cream and allow to cool at room temperature. Place in the fridge for 12 hours.

5. Pour the mixture into an ice cream maker and let it churn for 30–40 minutes.

6. Transfer the ice cream into a freezer-proof container and freeze for 12 hours.

7. Take the ice cream out of the freezer 15 minutes before serving to soften a little.

INDEX
&
MENUS

MENUS BY OCCASION

SPRING HOLIDAY MENU

Herring with potatoes and oil
Navarin of lamb with spring vegetables
Œufs à la neige

SUMMER HOLIDAY MENU

Gougères
Skate Grenobloise
Peach Melba

AUTUMN HOLIDAY MENU

Œufs en meurette (Eggs in red wine sauce)
Veal liver with grapes
Tarte Tatin

WINTER HOLIDAY MENU

Terrine of duck foie gras
Sweetbreads with morels
Chocolate profiteroles

END-OF-YEAR SPECIAL

Scallops au gratin
Tournedos Rossini
Dauphine potatoes
Chocolate soufflé

VEGGIE HOLIDAY MENU

Asparagus with Mousseline sauce
Cheese soufflé
Strawberry charlotte

WINTER MENU

*Potage parmentier (or Leek and
potato soup)*
Provençal beef cheek daube
Crêpes Suzette

SUMMER MENU

Pissaladière
Ratatouille
Sabayon with soft fruit

FOR A QUIET
WEEKEND

Roast chicken
French-style petits pois
Crème renversée

FAMILY SUNDAY
LUNCH

Leeks vinaigrette
Roast leg of lamb
Gratin dauphinois
Apple Tartlets

BISTRO-STYLE

Œufs mayonnaise
Knife-cut steak tartare
Frites
Chocolate mousse

FOR CHILDREN

Œufs cocotte with herbs
Croque-monsieur
Rice pudding

INDEX BY SUBJECT

INDEX BY SUBJECT

INDEX BY SUBJECT

INDEX BY SUBJECT

INDEX OF PRODUCE

INDEX OF STEP-BY-STEP PROCEDURES

INDEX OF HOMEMADE BASICS

INDEX OF RECIPES

THANKS TO...

Our elders!

The farmers, chefs, gourmets, weekend cooks as well as occasional weekday ones:
it's thanks to our elders that these recipes have become classics.

My cookery teachers at the École Ferrandi
who passed the importance of these uniting recipes on to me.

All the committed, enthusiastic cooks I come across.
For years I have watched you challenge, seek, encounter, try out, cook, taste and enjoy.
Here's a wink to Alain Ducasse, Alexandre Gauthier, Christian Constant,
Yves Camdeborde, Jacques Maximin, Olivier Nasti, Alain Passard, Yoni Saada,
Reine Sammut…

The Solar teams, under the management of Vincent Barbare.
Didier Férat and Diane Monserat, for their work and unwavering support.

Anne Bergeron, for her eye, which makes the recipes beautiful.
Vincent Amiel, culinary stylist high in vitamins and inspiration.
Lise Gaillaguet, my loyal make-up artist for so many years now.

My mate Jérôme Balland, the d'Artagnan of market gardening in the Piémont Vosgien region,
for his warm welcome and his love of Vosges farms.

Juliette Carré Bouquet for her kindness and charming welcome.

The Nord Compo team for the page layout, in particular Marie-Valentine Blond
for being so helpful.

My brilliant team, who are daily by my side, relentlessly.
Lucile Escourrou, Julien Amat, Julie Bernard, Stéphane Molé and Alain de La Rochère.

TF1 and Europe 1 for those encounters that make it possible for us to share the pleasure of
everyday cooking and much more.

My wife, for her fair, enlightening outlook, my son, for his honesty and sound taste,
my mother, who has always had a taste for authenticity.
My family and friends for all the lovely times in the kitchen and at the table.

You, my reader friends, who invite me to your table.
I am so happy about and proud of the bond between us.
It's now up to you to bring these recipes to life!

Finally, thanks to our vegetable gardeners.
The young ones, too!

First published in French, originally with the title:
La cuisine française pour tous

This edition published in 2024 by Hardie Grant Books,
an imprint of Hardie Grant Publishing

Hardie Grant Books (London)
5th & 6th Floors
52–54 Southwark Street
London SE1 1UN

Hardie Grant Books (Melbourne)
Building 1, 658 Church Street
Richmond, Victoria 3121

hardiegrantbooks.com

British Library Cataloguing-in-Publication Data. A catalogue record for this book
is available from the British Library.

Essentials of French Cuisine
ISBN: 978-1-78488-697-4

10 9 8 7 6 5 4 3 2 1

For the English edition:
Publishing Director: Kajal Mistry
Commissioning Editor: Kate Burkett
Senior Editor: Eila Purvis
Translator: Katherine Gregor
Typesettor: David Meikle
Proofreader: Kate Wanwimolruk
Indexer: Cathy Heath
Production Controller: Sabeena Atchia

Colour reproduction by p2d
Printed and bound in China by Leo Paper Products Ltd.